I0461441

ALIGNED
AT
HOME

HOW FENG SHUI AND HOLISTIC DESIGN CAN RESTORE YOUR ENERGY AND WELL-BEING

LISA MORTON

Aligned at Home: How Feng Shui and Holistic Design
Can Restore Your Energy and Well-Being
Published by Pure Living with Lisa Morton
Roanoke, Indiana

Copyright ©2025 by Lisa Morton and Pure Living
with Lisa Morton. All rights reserved.

All rights reserved. No part of this publication may be reproduced,
distributed, or transmitted in any form or by any means, including
photocopying, recording, or other electronic or mechanical methods,
without the prior written permission of the publisher, except
in the case of brief quotations embodied in critical reviews and
certain other noncommercial uses permitted by copyright law. For
information, contact the author at: purelivingwithlisa@gmail.com.

All images, logos, quotes, and trademarks included in
this book are subject to use according to trademark and
copyright laws of the United States of America.

ISBNs:
Paperback: 979-8-9933456-0-4
eBook: 979-8-9933456-1-1

BODY, MIND & SPIRIT / Feng Shui
HOUSE & HOME / Decorating & Furnishings

Cover and Interior design by Victoria Wolf,
wolfdesignandmarketing.com.

Edited by Gail Kerzner, The Savvy Red Pen, thesavvyredpen.com.

Printed in the United States of America.

PRAISE FOR THE BOOK

"I love *Aligned at Home* and highly recommend it. What began as Lisa's passion for design grew into a career that led her to projects in London, Paris, and around the world.

When she added feng shui to her practice, her clients raved not only about the results they were getting in their home but also in their lives. A few simple feng shui shifts would transform a client's destiny in wondrous ways. In this heartfelt book, Lisa provides immensely valuable feng shui information gained from her own professional life experiences that you can use to transform your destiny and turn your house into a home for the soul."

Denise Linn, Founder, Linn Academy, internationally renowned teacher of self-development, author of more than twenty books, including the bestseller *Sacred Space*.

"I really loved the nuggets of practical things presented. It felt very doable and something that I can try right away and see results."

Dr. Saloumeh DeGood, Clinical Psychologist, President, Sufi Psychology Association

"So many Feng Shui books are about rules and can leave the reader feeling confused, or worse, hopeless. Lisa has crafted a beautiful, heartfelt step-by step approach to create 'great feng shui' in your home. I absolutely recommend this book. *Aligned at Home* is a wonderful journey of Lisa's life, client success stories, and an uplifting experience to read."

LuAnn Cibik, Master Educator with Linn Academy, Founder, Inner Harmony

"*Aligned at Home* includes a lot of actionable steps. I don't feel like I need to revamp my whole space but can make small adjustments to shift the energy and have an impact."

Miranda Anderson, Professional Theater Stage Manager, Arts Educator

"Lisa's passion for feng shui is inspiring. Her actionable tips make transforming spaces easy and energizing. Living in a space that promotes health and happiness is within reach thanks to the wealth of information in Lisa's new book!"

Betsy Helmuth, Founder, Uploft Interior Design,
Author, *Affordable Interior Design*

"In *Aligned at Home*, Lisa Morton blends personal stories with professional wisdom to create a book that is both inspiring and practical. She makes Feng Shui and holistic design feel clear, empowering and immediately usable. More than a book, this is a guide to transforming your space, your life and yourself."

Margaret Kitch, Professional Astrologer,
Co-Host of *Celestial Curiosities* Podcast

"Lisa's transformation led her to be the thought leader she is today. I like the explanation and myth busting of Feng Shui. It opens the readers' eyes to the idea that they can start the process now in their homes and lives. *Aligned at Home* is a great gift for people buying new homes, retiring, moving locations, or just needing a fresh start. Lisa provides hope and practical tips on how readers can move forward."

Shannon Russell, Business Coach, Second Act Success,
Author, *Start Your Second Act*

"*Aligned at Home* has an approachable tone and pairs a topic that can feel intimidating (Feng Shui) with actions people are more comfortable with such as organizing and decorating."

Leslie Bailey, Business coach, Speaker,
Consultant to women entrepreneurs

To my husband, Don

My best friend, my everything, and occasionally, my furniture mover.

You've always believed in me, even when I doubted myself.

You were right. I *can* do anything I put my mind to
as long as I keep one foot in front of the other.

CONTENTS

FOREWORD

I AM SO EXCITED for the world to experience what I've been blessed to know firsthand: the quiet, radiant magic of Lisa Morton.

Before meeting Lisa, I had heard of Feng Shui. I thought it had something to do with rearranging furniture and maybe improving the "vibe" of a room, but I didn't get it. I didn't dismiss it, but I also wasn't drawn to it. Then I met Lisa, and my entire perception of Feng Shui and desire to learn about it changed immediately.

Our first meeting was for a design consultation. I was considering updating my podcast room. But it quickly became clear to me that I was being guided to something far deeper than fabric swatches and paint colors. Lisa was a gentle mystery who said very little about herself, yet it became clear she was connected to something beyond titles, education, and training.

I couldn't put my finger on it. Yet, I felt it—something ancient and wise. Her depth and gifts were cleverly disguised by her perfectly straight hair, smart glasses, and preppy style.

Until they weren't.

We met again for coffee, and I found myself doing what all podcasters do: asking questions and gently peeling back the layers of Lisa Morton. As she shared bits of her life story—some of which she now shares with you in this book—I felt something activate within me. I still didn't fully understand Feng Shui, and I didn't need to. I could feel it. I intuitively knew it went beyond this ancient art. I knew it was within Lisa and was connected to something she embodied during her years of unconventional training that she later married with Feng Shui. It was an essence that alchemized within her as she found her own path in interior design, Feng Shui, meditation, and energy work.

There was something profound here for me. And I suspect there is something here for you, too.

In fact, you're reading this, so there certainly is.

What followed was a home clearing and Feng Shui assessment that left me speechless. Lisa saw my home in a way I never had. She spoke of my home as if it were a living, breathing extension of me. I was fascinated. In the home clearing report, Lisa described architectural details she'd never laid eyes on. I can't explain how she does it, but through her training, education, magical gifts and wisdom, she sees beyond the walls.

The suggestions she made were specific, unconventional, and in some cases, hard for me to accept—like removing a mirror I loved that was styled perfectly according to interior design or replacing a coffee table I'd carefully chosen. But I promised to be teachable, so I joyfully complied. And within days of making these changes, the energetic shift was *undeniable*. I could feel it as soon as I re-entered my home. And that one room, my sitting room—the one I had never loved no matter how many times I updated the wallcoverings or furniture—became my favorite room in the house. It was warmer, more grounded, more alive. It felt like an embrace. Even my family, most of whom had no context for this kind of work, noticed the difference. Not with their eyes, but with their bodies. Their nervous systems relaxed. They wanted to be in that space. Guests gravitated to it, and I sat there daily after avoiding it for years. Even my five-year-old grandson said, "It's so relaxing and peaceful in here, Mimi!"

Soon, I was booking Lisa for my adult children, my clients, and my retreat attendees, quoting her, devouring her podcast and her Instagram posts. What I love is that I didn't need to explain her work. The impact spoke for itself. And the beautiful part? None of us need to understand Feng Shui intellectually to benefit from it. It only asks us to be open. And when Lisa adds her unique gifts to this ancient practice, the results are mind blowing and heart expanding. She creates resonance. Harmony. She helps you create a home that mirrors how you want to feel, live and love, while it simultaneously strums those chords within your internal home and heart. *Resonance.* Effortless flow.

I vividly remember one moment that will forever stay with me. My husband and I were navigating one of the most stressful periods of our lives, hemorrhaging money in a business that was rapidly becoming unsustainable. We called Lisa in for an emergency session. She had us tie red string to the pipes under every sink and place specific crystals and objects in precise areas of our home. It may sound strange—or even silly—but we did it. Three days later, with zero awareness of the connection, we walked into a meeting with our business partners and came out with a very clear peace, knowing that we needed to exit the business. The clarity came out of nowhere, as if a fog had lifted. We both knew that Lisa's energetic work had opened that door. It saved us hundreds of thousands of dollars. The decision confused everyone around us, yet we had so much clarity around it. It was for certain, a decision that nearly a year out, we can confidently say saved us not just truckloads of money, but months of stress and anxiety.

Lisa Morton is a combination of Yoda and Mary Poppins. Her presence—and her work—is transformational and so magical. And this book? It's the same. Plus icing. And sprinkles. It's not just a guide to Feng Shui. It's not just a beautifully organized, practical handbook full of usable tips and practical advice. This book is Lisa. It's her essence on the pages: calm, clear, grounded, quietly powerful, effervescent, and surprisingly personal. She doesn't just tell you how to move a chair or place a mirror; she takes you by the hand and brings you into her story. And by doing so, she gently calls you back to your own.

This book will shift the way you see your home. But more than that, it will shift the way you see yourself. Because our homes are not separate from us. They are us. They hold our patterns, our histories, our fear and our aspirations. They reveal where we are stuck and where we are ready to expand. And with Lisa as your guide, you'll learn to read those signals with new eyes—and create a space that truly supports who you're becoming.

So, take a breath. Open your heart. And step in.

You're in for something special.

— Jill Herman
Certified Trauma Informed Life Coach
Host of *Be You*, A Top 100 Podcast

PREFACE

I WAS A GUEST ON A PODCAST when the host asked me a thought-provoking question: "If your life were a book, what chapter would you be in?"

I paused, searching for the perfect answer, but deep down, I knew there was only one true response: "The best chapter ever." Not the beginning, not the end, but somewhere in the middle, where growth meets possibility. It's that exhilarating place where you realize how far you've come, with wisdom and experience, yet you know there's still so much more to explore, create, experience, and achieve.

When I was younger, I thought life meant clocking in and counting the minutes until it was time to go home. I never imagined I'd carve out a career path that's been anything but ordinary—full of twists and turns, countless lessons, and unforgettable experiences.

I always thought I'd write a book. People told me I should. But this was not the book I thought I'd be delivering to you, though. In fact, for the first three months of writing, I was writing with a completely different intention. That version was solely focused on Feng Shui and more of an informational book. I then realized there are enough of those books out there. This book needed to be filled with experiences, stories, and lots of soul.

Intuition took over, and the writer in me began to shift. I began to feel an immense sense of healing in my writing, and I started to love writing more than I ever thought possible. It became slow, beautiful, meditative, and intuitive rather than a task or chore.

Years ago, I went to a psychic fair with my friend, Lindsey. I was hoping to snag some beautiful new rock specimens; however, we ended up talking to a woman who was offering psychic readings. I'll admit I wasn't sold. I'd had my share of readings like this done over the years and have found some interesting connections and confirmations with some, but this one? Not so much. Oh well, I'd already paid her and thought I might as well continue listening.

She told me that one day I'd write a book. She told me the name of the book (which is not the name of this book, but I may use it someday). She also told me writing this book would be a wonderful experience. Then she added, "I want you to go over to the vendor table across the room who has books for sale and look for a book with a green binding. You'll need this book to support your writing."

Uh, ok. I decided I had nothing to lose and might find another interesting book on rocks and crystals. Sure enough, the first book I saw had a green spine. The title? *Writing as a Way of Healing.*

Of course, I had to buy it, but it sat on my bookshelf gathering dust for years—unopened until a year ago when it whispered, "The time is now."

The book you're holding shares my personal journey and highlights some favorite stories.

I share my experiences of living what I thought was my dream life, only to find myself sinking into a season of deep struggle. The practices in this book not only guided me through my own healing but also helped me create a life and home that truly support who I am—and they can do the same for you.

I also guide you through the transformative power of Feng Shui and holistic design. You'll learn how to clear clutter, harness the energy of your space, and make intentional changes to foster balance, health, and true joy. This is your guide to creating a space that nurtures both your lifestyle and your spirit, your guide to feeling more aligned at home.

My goal? To share practical, easy-to-digest tools that reveal the subtle yet powerful ways your home may be influencing your life and well-being. My hope is that as you read, you begin to view your home with new lenses—that you view it not as something separate from your life but as space actively shaping your energy, your emotions, and your sense of possibility.

Even as an interior designer, I didn't fully realize just how much the small, seemingly insignificant details like the placement of a chair, the color of a room, or the clutter in a forgotten corner could impact the energy of a space. And how that energy could create a ripple effect on how I felt in my body. Only after facing burnout, I began making changes in my home for the sake of my *own* well-being that it all really clicked. I didn't redesign my home to be trendy or beautiful; I redesigned it to be healing.

A line in Gay Hendrick's book, The Big Leap, stopped me cold: "My mess became my message." The deeper I leaned into healing and alignment, starting with my home, the more I saw how many others were quietly craving the same thing: a home that didn't just look good but felt deeply supportive. A home that helped them return to themselves.

This book is born from that realization. Aligning your home is not about perfection or beauty, it's about connection, an invitation to make even the smallest shift in your environment with strong intention and to watch how that shift echoes throughout the rest of your life.

CHAPTER 1

When Your Home
Speaks Back

YOUR HOME ISN'T JUST a physical structure; it's a living, breathing mirror of your inner world reflecting your subconscious beliefs, habits, goals, and dreams. The connection between your home and your life runs deeper than you might imagine.

THE CONNECTION BETWEEN
YOU AND YOUR HOME

Look around: Are the countertops cluttered with paperwork and random dishes to sort? Is the ice maker leaking, lightbulbs burned out, a fine layer of dust settling on top of surfaces you haven't touched in weeks? These aren't just signs of a busy life; they're signs that reflect what may be happening inside of you. This can happen to all of us, but you can shift away from this overwhelm by becoming more intentional about your space. By taking this experience on, you can unlock the ability to shape your environment in a way that both nurtures and aligns with your best self. You'll feel more calm, more clear, more grounded, connected, and joyful.

Many people think of their space as simply four walls, some windows and a few doors— nothing more than a place to crash at the end of a long day. If that's how you feel now, that's okay. You're not alone. But what if your home could be more than that?

My intention is to help you open your eyes to the possibilities our homes can provide. Our home environment influences who we are, what we're about, and where we're going. The connection between your home and your life runs deep. In *Sacred Space,* my favorite Denise Linn book, she shares, "Homes, like people, are nourished by how we hold them in our hearts."

Your home is also a reflection of your subconscious beliefs, shaping your thoughts, emotions, and everyday choices. Imagine walking into a living room, where the furniture is arranged awkwardly and the space feels cramped and uninviting. Without realizing it, this setup could be reinforcing some subconscious beliefs that you feel stuck, your relationships feel disconnected, and you aren't sure of your future. Every room in your home, every object, trinket, and even furniture arrangement contributes to the energy in your home shaping your life.

Now imagine the same living room and rearranging the space to promote flow. You move the sofa so you can see the door, you clear the clutter, and you add some pretty accent pillows and a chunky throw. The energy shifts, and you can feel it. This space encourages clarity and comfort, and before you know it, you're inviting friends over for a cup of tea. By recognizing and fostering this connection, you can design a space that not only supports, but also elevates your life's journey, aligning your surroundings with your goals and overall well-being. Maybe you're ready to take on that side hustle candle making business or you're inspired to start a book club.

If you're feeling a little hesitant about diving into this book, I get it. It could stir up more than you're ready for. Trust me, I understand how life can feel overwhelmingly busy. That's why I created my podcast, *Feng Shui Living: Tips for Busy Women*. Demands of work, getting enough exercise, supporting mental health, eating enough veggies, and keeping the family on track is a lot! But here's the thing: You don't need to overhaul your entire life to make meaningful changes. This isn't a detox. It's about slowing down, taking time to observe, and creating intentional steps forward, one small shift at a time.

LET'S EXPLORE

This is the perfect time for you to snag a new notebook or journal and a pen you love.

Before you make any changes to your home, let's explore your space with your senses.

Take a few minutes and head outside for some fresh air. Feel the breeze blow across your face. Notice the coolness of your breath as it enters your nose and the warmth as it exits. What do you hear? Birds? The distant hum of traffic? Leaves rustling in the breeze? What do you smell? Fresh cut grass? Someone's morning coffee? What colors do you see? Breathe and connect to the nature around you and get clear headed.

3

When you're ready, head back inside, and walk through the front door as if you were a guest visiting for the first time. You've never been here before and don't know anything about the people who live here.

Think about these questions:

- Where do your eyes land when you enter? Are you drawn to the grand fireplace?

- What draws you in? Maybe the jewel-toned furniture feels particularly striking.

- What do you hear? A cat's meow or clock ticking?

- What do you smell? Fresh flowers or wet dog?

- What colors do you see? Soft, muted colors or bold, vibrant hues?

- What do you enjoy looking at? A collection of travel photos and some family heirlooms?

- If your eyes are pulled in a specific direction, what's there? A spectacular painting on the wall, bright natural lighting filling the room?

Now close your eyes and just breathe. What does the energy in the home feel like? What's the vibe?

How would you describe it to someone?

- Calming and relaxing?

- Peaceful and grounding?

- Active and busy?

- Disjointed and depressing?

- Cheerful and playful?

Now that you've taken on this experiment, you've had your first taste of exploring your home with fresh eyes. Maybe you had an "ah-ha" moment realizing just how your home is impacting you. Ready to go deeper? Let's begin.

CHAPTER 2

Chasing the Dream
... and Catching It

NATURE LOVER—THAT'S ME

My favorite time of day is early morning just before sunrise. I love relaxing and sitting outside in the swing on our rural property, coffee in hand, while the dogs roam, sniffing out the trails of deer and other nighttime visitors. There's something so incredibly peaceful, almost magical, about this place. The sky slowly shifts from night to day as the first rays of sunlight peek out over the treetops. It's a quiet, gentle, grounding moment before the world fully wakes up, and I get to soak it all in.

Life was not always this peaceful and slow. But my experiences have shaped and reminded me of who I truly am at my core, a deep lover of nature drawn to its beauty and rhythm.

IN LOVE WITH INTERIOR SPACES

My story begins like this: I grew up on a farm in rural Iowa in the '80s and '90s. We had one "decorator" in town, who designed my grandmother's new draperies. I remember hearing about it and dreaming of what it would be like when they were installed. I thought this job seemed fascinating. Touching luxurious damasks and silks and selecting trims sounded amazing. Could I do that?

I was an avid fan of the TV show, *Designing Women.* What was better than a show about female designers bantering about their lives and work while spending their days in a gorgeous Southern home? I'd constantly rotate from wanting to be like the dramatic Delta Burke to the hilarious Annie Pots or even all-business Dixie Carter. By this time, I'd already begged my mom to let me sponge paint my bedroom blue, was rearranging my bedroom weekly, and spending hours sketching rooms, drawing floor plans and even doodling in and "improving" the images in B*etter Homes & Gardens* with my markers. I knew I loved interior spaces but wasn't sure if interior design could be a real career.

Fast forward several years, and I'd graduated with a degree in interior design, moved to St. Louis, and was working as a design assistant for a residential design firm. While it's vital to learn the technical aspects in school, I learned the most from being in my clients' homes. My favorite experiences were tagging along with the principal designer to job sites. I relished the opportunity to be in someone's home and take in the environment. I'd wonder, "What made them buy this? Why do they like this piece?" I wasn't judging the homes, just enjoying the opportunity to see them, meet the owners, see how they felt, used, and moved throughout their spaces.

I also enjoyed seeing how clients felt renewed when our project was complete. I remember Mrs. Mecham, a client with a gorgeous craftsman home, standing back and admiring the newly installed wall sconces. I could see the thrill in her eyes. Most clients were overjoyed and showed a renewed energy I loved. Creating beautiful and functional spaces was important, and I could witness it firsthand.

MY CAREER TAKES OFF

While I loved this work, I kept hoping for more. I knew there was more I could do. I just wasn't sure what. Maybe I needed to look in another direction?

That's when I landed what I thought was my dream job designing private jet interiors. You read that right! Yes, it's a real job, who knew? I knew nothing about that type of work, but the company was impressed with my eagerness to learn.

For several years, I designed custom-designed jets for celebrities, global executives, dignitaries, and even sports teams. These green aircraft came straight from the factory as hollow shells. I got to dream up beautiful and unique schemes and plans, and our talented craftspeople could build them.

I traveled the world for this job. The first time I went to Turkey, Istanbul felt so bizarre, but after a few trips, I grew to love it. The idea of a city spanning two continents was mind-boggling. I remember riding the Tube in London for the first time and watching the Eiffel Tower light up at night with its beautiful sparkle. I wasn't just a farm girl from a small town in Iowa anymore. I had made it into the world and believed I belonged there.

Our clients were a mixed bag. The American clients were mostly polite and just anxious to get their plane delivered. Most of my international clients were fantastic. I'll never forget when our team was invited to a Passover meal at a client's personal home in Tel Aviv. They were so welcoming and inviting, and the food was amazing!

I experienced moments that felt right out of a movie, like when I was scheduled to meet a Paris-based designer for a collaborative project, and the meeting got canceled at the last minute because he fell as he was leaving the Hèrmes store. I flew all the way to Paris just to have to turn around and fly back home to St. Louis. But I took it in stride. Did I know a single word in French? No. Were there translation apps then? No. I survived and was pretty proud of myself.

Then there was a prominent Texas lawyer and his wife who came to our facility to select materials. She was so fashionable and confident. I thought, I *want to be like that; she has it all together.* She was a successful interior designer in Houston, and we enjoyed working together on their plane. Designing for planes was a different beast: strict safety codes, limited material options, the necessity for everything to be lightweight and flame retardant. The result of this collaboration project? A gorgeous plane filled with luxurious textures, along with their favorite delicate taupe and soft purple colors.

Designing private jets was everything I had once dreamed about—and more. I had chased the dream and caught it, living a life filled with travel, luxury, and once-in-a-lifetime opportunities. For a girl who grew up on an Iowa farm, it felt almost surreal. I had stepped into a world I never imagined I could belong to, and for a time, it was thrilling.

CHAPTER 3:

The Shine Wears Off

It was all glamorous and fun, until it wasn't. I was travelling internationally *and* domestically attending client meetings, meetings with reps, and approving the materials for plane interiors such as the wood veneer, leather for seats, cabinetry, and carpeting.

I'd buy concert tickets or make dinner plans only to cancel because someone was flying in from Africa for a last-minute meeting. I also took "vacation days" that turned into work marathons. Once, I visited my sister in rural Iowa and needed to go to a gas station to make phone calls because there was poor cell service at her house at the time. I spent half my day making calls at that gas station. She was upset with me, and I felt just awful.

THE PRICE OF PERFECTIONISM

The perfectionist in me *loved* this job. My clothing was fashionable and tasteful, and I tried to convey just the right message: I had it all together and looked great doing it. Did I regret the beautiful heels I'd wear even when my feet ached? Heck no! They look so good! My presentations were sharp, and each design had solid intent. My cubicle was structured perfectly; each project file was organized beyond belief. I was in constant contact with the workrooms and reps, provided extra schemes or materials nearly on command, and adored being given the special projects. My bosses knew I would do everything in my power to ensure a perfect creation. The mere thought of making a mistake was crippling. I couldn't be the cause of an issue. I couldn't be human; I had to be flawless.

I remember thinking, *I don't know how long I can do this.* Then regret set in. *This is the coolest job in the world. How dare I think that way?*

The private aviation industry really took off in 2007—pun intended. Clients were buying and selling planes left and right. I'd have to start all over with a new client, creating a totally new interior after spending eight months working on a selected design. Clients requested outrageous designs, even though I was already using materials such as goat skin, gold and silver leaf, mother of pearl, and stingray. Once we even designed a project with backlit onyx . . . in the bathroom! Did I mention the china and flatware? Oh, how I loved opening the beautiful Hermés orange boxes and the Baccarat crystal shipments. A highlight of my day was placing each piece carefully on the table while drooling over the collection. I'd imagine myself sipping tea from the delicate cup and saucer.

One of the most trying projects involved a custom, hand-tufted carpet—a gorgeous pastel blue with navy blue and green accents.

Literally, a man stood on a platform in a factory and tufted the entire rug. What a thing of beauty! But during installation, a single tufted line measured one-eighth inch off from the engineered drawing. No one could see it; no one would even know. But it wasn't an exact match to the drawings. This meant the entire $20,000 carpet had to be completely scrapped and remade before it was accepted—not once but twice!

I started to notice that my nerves were spent when I'd get home from my hour-long commute at the end of the day. Eventually, I found myself walking into my house and immediately curling up on the couch. I'd throw a blanket over my head and begin to cry. I didn't know why. I just didn't feel well and didn't know what to do or what was wrong with me. I was miserable and ashamed. *What on earth was going on?* I tried to hide my stress. On the outside, I looked composed, but on the inside, I was unraveling.

I've always been the type of person to find a solution if there's an issue. There's no giving up; you do your research, readjust, and keep moving forward. I began seeing a therapist, meditating, and practicing yoga. While I believe these actions supported me in one way or another, I knew something was missing. I continued to dig, exploring everything from exercise to Reiki healing and everything in between. Where would I ever find the answer?

CHAPTER 4

The Day Everything Shifted

BEFORE THINGS GOT BETTER, they got worse. The physical symptoms started occurring more: sleepless nights, constant irritability, digestive issues, back spasms. The funny thing is I didn't think it was at all related. I simply thought stress was just worrying too much and the feeling would eventually go away. I started getting a weekly massage but found myself even more overwhelmed after taking that time for myself instead of working.

UNDER THE WEIGHT OF IT ALL

The day I hit the tipping point, I was in a client meeting sitting in a large conference room around an oval table with colleagues and the client's representatives. The project had not gone as planned, mostly because the client couldn't make decisions. I provided them with hundreds of samples for consideration, each documented carefully (of course). Unfortunately, the consultant decided to use me as the punching bag and blame me for the issues. He yelled across the room, "We didn't receive any materials to select from, and this is your fault!"

Sweat rolled down my back as I heard the lies and accusations. My heart started beating harder and harder. I wondered if the woman sitting next to me could hear it. I certainly could. How embarrassing!

After this meeting, sheer panic became all too familiar. While I continued to be the "perfect designer," I knew I needed to explore my health. Something was going on, and I had to get to the bottom of it.

On a cold, icy day in January, I took the morning off from work and bundled up to see my doctor. I went to this appointment fearing that I was going to have a heart attack. After an examination and several questions, she looked at me and said, "Sweetie, I think you have anxiety."

What? Me? I knew I was a "worrier" but didn't realize this is what anxiety felt like.

From there, things got worse. I was doing everything I knew to do for support and was still in therapy, walking and meditating without relief. I'd lie to my team and tell them I had to walk to another workroom to check a sample just as a panic attack was coming on. I'd sit in my car crying hysterically, then wonder if they were upset I was gone. I was overcome with guilt and wondered, *Am I letting them down?* It was a vicious cycle. Fear, Guilt, Shame, Guilt.

Sometimes, I'd hide in the design closet surrounded by luxurious swatches. The design supply closet became my panic attack closet. One day, our assistant, Maddie, found me. I was mortified. I just started sobbing more and ran out to my car. I didn't even bother to go back in but calmed down enough to drive home. Things *had* to change.

While my team and bosses were trying to support me as best they could (I'd finally swallowed my pride and fessed up to what was happening), and my husband was valiantly doing everything possible he could, I knew something had to give.

THE FINAL STRAW

The last straw was when I began driving down the freeway to work every morning thinking, *If I just graze the cement barrier separating the lanes I'd damage my car but wouldn't have to go to work.*

I didn't want to hurt myself but couldn't stand the thought of being there. But how could I leave them hanging? Fear, Guilt, Shame, Guilt.

I finally told my team and my husband after chats with my therapist that this journey had to end. What in the world was I going to do? I hadn't a clue. This work was my life. I didn't even remember how to do other design work. So, I decided to do what anyone in my shoes would do: I left my job and then proceeded to get a haircut and got bangs.

I went home and slept for four days straight with my dog, Bear, at my side. I couldn't leave the house. The depression sank in deep, really deep. Add in the feeling of shame for "not being able to cut it" and having to leave. I couldn't stand to look in the mirror. The reflection frightened me. Even my weekly trip to the grocery store a block away was a struggle.

When my therapist called me a perfectionist, I thought, *Me? Perfect?* I didn't understand that my perfectionism isn't about being perfect but rather about being "just-so" or what I "expected." To challenge me, she gave me a task: wear mismatched socks to the grocery store. While no one would have even seen them under my pant legs, I spent days debating it. I finally did it and didn't die. I thought someday I'd be at the store and die; I'd be lying there, and random people would just be stepping over me as they looked for the cereal aisle. Yes, bizarre but that's what was in my head in my moment of panic.

If you've ever found yourself crying in your car, hiding your pain behind your profession, or wondering how you got so far from yourself, I see you. I was you. But this is where your journey home begins.

CHAPTER 5

The Spark Returns

OVER THE NEXT SEVERAL MONTHS, I slowly began venturing out of the house more. Little by little, I started to feel more human and less like an alien. My husband and I talked about making some changes. Ironically, he'd just been approached about a job in Cleveland, Ohio. He grew up there, and his whole family was still in the area. What a comforting idea! Before I knew it, the semi was loaded with our belongings, and we were en route toward our fresh start.

REINVENTING HOME AND SELF

Maybe I was naive. I thought I'd had an impressive resume and portfolio, but it was 2010, and no one was hiring. So, I decided to start my own residential design business. I'd done some freelance work with great results, so why not? I also worked part-time for a custom closet manufacturer, and I knew I'd get impressive leads for my work there too.

But being an entrepreneur is not for the faint of heart. Sure, I was able to control my schedule when I was having a rough few days (the anxiety and depression was still hanging heavy), but trying to grow and get my name out as well as connect with the trades and suppliers kept me busy. I found myself once again in a client's home exploring what made them tick. I found a little sparkle again.

I also started exploring my space through a different lens. Why did I make certain choices in my space? How did that make me feel? I began ordering books on creating healthy homes and reading about Feng Shui. The books were fascinating, but I was just sure Feng Shui was nothing more than superstition. But honestly, at this point, I was up for trying anything. Plus, every book seemed to say something different. How can that be? Still, something in me kept turning the pages. I didn't know it yet, but I was beginning to read the language of energy.

Continuing to struggle with my well-being, I had recently taken on some alternative approaches to self-care, including Reiki healing sessions. I couldn't believe the positive physical effects of this work, so I decided to train in this healing modality myself. I was fascinated and became a Reiki Master. I never intended to do it on others: just myself—maybe my dog. I discovered I was no longer chasing something outside of me. I was listening for something within.

One day it hit me. If my body has this energy field, then my surroundings must have energy too. Oh yeah, that's like Feng Shui! Maybe it's time to explore more deeply.

CHAPTER 6

The Ancient Art That Changed Everything

AFTER READING BOOK AFTER BOOK on Feng Shui, I found myself both fascinated and frustrated. Each book seemed to contradict the last. I loved the concept, but the confusion left me craving clarity. I knew it was time to find a real mentor.

THE PATH TO PERSONAL SPACE

I began studying one-on-one with an incredible teacher who taught The Form School approach. She explained the different "schools" or "sects" of Feng Shui and that each had the same goal but different approaches. The Form School (the original form of Feng Shui) emphasizes the importance of considering natural features such as landforms, mountains, and rivers when designing and arranging a space, recognizing the influence these had on the surrounding environment. I enjoyed learning from her—especially because of my deep-rooted love of nature, but again, I knew I was looking for something deeper, more personal.

One evening while scrolling online, I stumbled upon a school that taught something called Instinctive Feng Shui™, which has roots in Form school and BTB (Black Sect Feng Shui, a more western approach). It also has a component that focuses on the individual's needs and their deepest self-desires for their environment. These needs and desires are accessed through a Synchro-Alignment™ process, a guided meditation where the consultant supports the client in uncovering what their soul is craving.

This process and style of Feng Shui was created by Denise Linn, known for her deep understanding of native tribal rituals and practices as well as connection to her own Native American heritage. Her approach honors the traditions while also understanding that we're a melting pot of interesting and unique individuals, each living our lives differently. One client may have deep spiritual beliefs that they want to implement into their home. The next client may live in a multi-generational home with several people living under one roof. Each home requires vastly different things.

Denise also urges people to understand the importance of creating a healthy home free of chemicals and toxins—with fresh air to breathe and as much connection to nature as possible. Denise calls this work Interior Alignment®. It felt like the clouds had parted. Sign me up!

A JOURNEY TO MASTERY

I dove in, and in fall 2014, I completed my Interior Alignment® Instinctive Feng Shui™ certification under LuAnn Cibik's guidance. At the same time, I also received my Seven Star Blessing Space Clearing™ certification from her. The experience was transformative. I felt like I had finally come home. I felt understood, with a deeper connection to life and to spirit.

My new obsession became implementing and exploring this work with my interior design clients. Some loved it; some didn't understand it, but I knew I now had the knowledge to create powerful spaces for them. I focused on designing environments that could help them relax at the end of a busy day with the right grounding finishes and patterns and help their children sleep better by using more natural colors and materials.

In 2018, I furthered my studies to become an advanced practitioner of Instinctive Feng Shui™ and trained in Medicine Wheel Feng Shui™. This approach covers Native American beliefs, practices, and rituals and how to use them as a form of home energy alignment. In summer 2024, I rounded out my studies to become a Master Teacher of Interior Alignment® Feng Shui and Space Clearings which was a huge "bucket list" item of mine. I now have the honor of teaching others how to perform this powerful work.

Feng Shui isn't just about rearranging furniture; it's truly centuries of practice and careful implementation. My favorite aspect of this work is the ability to add "cues" into homes. Say you want to manifest your dream job or you're wishing for the love of your life. Through careful design and Feng Shui adjustments, we can bring those desires to fruition. Sure, some people might think this sounds "woo" or too "out there," but it's really science! It's energy! And it works!

Denise Linn often compares Feng Shui to adjusting an old rabbit ear antenna. Sometimes, all it takes is a tiny tweak for everything to come into focus. It's a reminder that creating balance and harmony in your home doesn't require a complete remodel or major changes. Sometimes, it's the smallest adjustments that make the most significant difference.

So, let me ask you. Are you ready to make shifts in your life?

What are *your* dreams and wishes? Be specific! This is your invitation to get clear. Not safe or small—but bold. What are you ready to bring into your life? Want to start your dream business? Build your dream home? Run a marathon? Get engaged? Add to your family?

Now is the time to get really clear on what you want. The more clarity you have moving forward, the easier and more rewarding the outcome will be. Have no fear, if you're wondering how to make these tweaks, keep reading, I'm with you all the way. Let's explore how by getting intentional.

CHAPTER 7

Beyond Beautiful: Intentional Design for Well-Being

HOME INTERIOR DESIGN as we once knew is evolving, and the future looks nothing like the past. Don't get me wrong, I've loved my career in design and have so much admiration for the incredible work that many talented designers continue to do. But times are changing. What mattered to previous generations doesn't always align with what we value today or what future generations will prioritize.

A HEALTHIER APPROACH

For me, health and well-being are at the top of the list, and I know I'm not alone. Our awareness of how our environment affects our physical and mental health has grown, and younger generations are taking it even further. They're asking questions about sourcing, sustainability, carbon footprints, and how the materials we bring into our homes impact their wellbeing and their families. The Eco-Friendly Furniture Market is projected to grow from USD 878.05 million in 2023 to an estimated USD 1640 million by 2032[1] Also, DexDecor notes that the Green building materials market is expected to reach $425 billion by 2026.[2] This shift is exciting, and it's inspiring to see design becoming more about creating spaces that truly support a better way of living.

You may think of an interior designer as someone who sketches plans, pulls fabric and tile samples, and creates beautiful interiors. But have you ever heard of holistic interior design? This approach is about these same processes but creating spaces that nurture your mind, body, and spirit. It's much more than just making a home look beautiful (while that's a bonus). The focus is about aligning your environment with your energy, intentions, and well-being. By combining traditional interior design principles along with elements such as Feng Shui (the ancient art and science of arrangement), biophilia (that inner craving to connect to natural elements), and mindfulness, it ensures that every aspect of your home supports your lifestyle and helps you thrive emotionally, mentally, and physically. I consider it to be designed with a healthy dose of heart and purpose.

---

1   "Market Overview," https://www.credenceresearch.com/report/eco-friendly-furniture-market.

2   "Interior Design Statistics for 2024," https://www.dexdecor.com/interior-design-statistics-for-2024/.

YOUR HOME, YOUR STORY

Now if all this sounds a bit overwhelming, let's start with some fun. Below are some ideas for creating a space that truly honors you and your family's interests and personalities. After all, isn't that *really* what our home is all about?

1. Family Decor

Are you taking a photography class or attempting watercolor for the first time? Display your art proudly! Your kids' artwork might not be museum ready, but go ahead and decorate with your favorites. Recently, I helped a client with her children's artwork. We framed several pieces in a sleek black modern frame. The quality framing made the pieces look stylish, and kids were so excited to see their creations on the walls. Plus, clutter artwork stayed off the fridge, which was a stressful area for this client. What can you display to showcase your family's talents?

2. Heirlooms

People often keep family heirlooms boxed up in closets for "safe keeping." If you have treasured pieces you've inherited that you love, use them as decoration in your home. They can be effective conversation starters and significant memories of your family history and heritage. The key is to ensure you truly feel connected to the item, not that you feel obligated to display them. Use a beautiful dish for trinkets, opt for the vintage glassware at your next holiday dinner, or wear the vintage costume jewelry on a fun lunch date.

3. Travel Collections

Find a theme or collection that you can gather while on your travels. I once worked with a family that would bring a seashell back from every beach vacation. We created a unique display on their bookshelf, and their kids love hearing stories from the trips. Do you have a beautiful scarf collection from your trips? Display them. Maybe you collect coffee mugs on your travels; set up a vignette in your kitchen.

4. Shop Local

I love to shop local and support local businesses. Pop into your favorite boutiques and art galleries and see what catches your eye. Think beyond just wall art; look for sculptures, pottery, glass, and carved wood. Celebrate your community by decorating with pieces crafted by local artisans and craftsmen.

Keep a card, brochure or website on hand. Visitors often ask me for more information on the crafter or creator of some of my favorite pieces.

—Lisa

Your style and decor can speak volumes about who you are. Let your space highlight those unique stories and passions that make you and your family special. After all, being *you* matters most.

CHAPTER 8

The Power of Daily Rituals

DEVELOPING ROUTINES

A routine is a set of actions or behaviors performed regularly, often in a specific order. Routines tend to serve practical purposes such as organization and efficiency.

James Clear explains in his book *Atomic Habits*, "You can train yourself to link a particular habit with a particular context" and that starting or changing a habit is easier when you're in new surroundings. "When you step outside your normal environment, you leave your behavioral biases behind."[3]

---

3   James Clear, *Atomic Habits*, (Avery, Penguin House, 2018), 88.

This resonates deeply with me, not only as someone who works with the energy of space, but also as someone who has witnessed how a simple shift in your environment can really spark transformation in your life.

Have you ever found it easier to start journaling in a fresh notebook with a new pen? Or noticed that you sleep better after buying new bedding? That's not a coincidence. When we shift our environment, even slightly, it's almost like we create energetic permission for something new. A cozy chair with a throw blanket can become your special morning reading spot. A tidy, organized kitchen counter can inspire you to cook a delicious meal instead of ordering takeout. Even lighting a candle at the same time each evening can signal your nervous system to wind down. Burning incense every morning while making my morning cup of coffee became a sacred time for me. This small shift of lighting my favorite Nag-Champa incense each day inspired me to slow down, to sip my coffee, and take in all the flavors. I'd get quiet, look out across the pond, watch the ducks land in the water, and take in the glorious colors of the morning sky.

When you intentionally design your space to support the version of yourself, your routines and habits feel less like effort and more like pretty magical alignment. You're not forcing change; you're inviting it in with open arms.

EVERYDAY HABITS, LASTING EFFECTS

Habits, on the other hand, are more automated behaviors shaped by repetition over time. While routines generally serve a purpose and are more goal-oriented, habits tend to become ingrained without much thought. They then begin shaping our lives in subtle ways. So much of what we do each day is guided by these deeply ingrained habits. It's almost amazing how most of our thoughts, words, and actions unfold without actual thought or intention.

Ready to explore this deeper? Let's shine a light on some of these unconscious behaviors.

The last time you bought a new piece of art or a throw pillow, you probably smiled every time you walked by, appreciating the fresh addition to your space. But over time, that initial excitement fades, and the piece quietly blends into the background, almost as if it's no longer there. You might occasionally admire it but not like when you first acquired it. Yet, even if you're not consciously noticing it, the item remains significant. On a subconscious level, you're still connecting with and responding to it.

A family friend gifted me a pink floral hand-painted vase for my wedding. Honestly, I didn't care for it. I'm sure the artist took a lot of time crafting it, but it wasn't my style and didn't feel like me. For months, I'd walk past the vase and felt guilty that I didn't love it or even really like it. I was frustrated about what to do with it. Instead of the item bringing me joy, reminding me of my wedding, I was annoyed believing I had to keep it.

Shortly after, while my mom was visiting, she mentioned how pretty she thought it was. Ah-ha! She needed this vase! I was happy to give it to her because it fits her style and home decor—and I no longer wanted the feelings of guilt for not liking it. I replaced it with a spectacular hand-blown glass bowl I absolutely loved. It complimented our color scheme, and everything felt like it fell into place, plus I simply adored the artist who created it.

Our home interiors and belongings are constantly shaping and influencing who we are. Are they filled with things that make you smile, or as my teacher, LuAnn Cibik, says "juice up your life"? If your space is filled with more of those items that you just habitually stroll past and don't even notice, slow down and take a look. Are they still serving you?

WHAT IS YOUR HOME SAYING?

Take a moment with this journal prompt:

If your home were a metaphor for your
life, what would it be saying?

COMMITTING TO YOUR HOME

Committing to your home is about more than just choosing beautiful furniture, accessories or the perfect paint color. It's a mindset shift that prioritizes intentional design that aligns your space with your deepest desires and aspirations. When you dedicate your time and energy to cultivating an environment that reflects who you are and supports your journey, your home transforms from a place you simply live in into a sanctuary that truly fuels you. Betsy Helmuth writes in *Affordable Interior Design*, "Committing to a home is just like committing to a partner. Whether you rent or own, whether you have a steady boyfriend/girlfriend or a husband/wife, you gotta love the one you're with."[4] She explains that just as you choose a partner, you choose your home for a reason. Rather than focusing on flaws, remember what made you fall in love with it.

---

4   Betsy Helmuth, *Affordable Interior Design*, (Skyhorse, 2019), 16.

This commitment isn't a one-time thing; it's an ongoing relationship that grows and evolves with you, responding to the seasons of your life and the shifts in your lifestyle and priorities. Often, it can take a few steps for a client to fall in love with their home again. Sometimes it just takes remembering and a few adjustments to reset.

REMEMBER

Routine vs. Habit

A routine is a regular sequence of actions done in a set order.

A habit is a behavior repeated so often that it becomes automated.

CAROL FELL OUT OF LOVE WITH HER HOME

Twenty years ago, my client, Carol, had poured her heart into building her dream home. Every detail had been carefully chosen, from the sprawling open concept layout to the intricate custom woodwork. For years, her home was her sanctuary, a place filled with laughter and many memories. But as time passed, life shifted. Her two kids grew up and moved out, she no longer enjoyed being the host of events and holidays, and she didn't feel the connection to her home anymore.

Carol called me and told me tearfully, "I don't love my home anymore." She described how she felt disconnected from the space she had once loved. The rooms felt too big, too empty, and too outdated for her current life.

When I arrived, I could see it right away. The house was still beautiful, but it wasn't aligned with who Carol was anymore. I explained that our homes are living, evolving spaces, and just like us, they need attention to grow and change. Her adult children's rooms were still the same from when they lived there. Her art studio in the basement was dusty and unused. Cabinets and closets were jam packed with party supplies— everything from serving ware to plasticware, punch bowls, water carafes, platters, and more that she hadn't used in years.

We started by digging into what Carol needed *now*. I asked her to share how she wanted to feel in her home. Her eyes lit up as she described her desire for warmth and comfort. She wanted a space that felt inviting for quiet mornings with coffee and cozy evenings with a few close friends for a glass of wine. The massive family gatherings and parties she used to host no longer interested her. I asked if she wanted to paint again in her studio, and her eyes brightened. Yes, she did, but something held her back.

Using the Feng Shui Bagua Map, a tool to locate various energy centers of the home, we identified areas that needed attention. In the large living room, we introduced some softer elements such as plush throws, a textural rug, and pretty lamps to set the tone for cozy coffee moments and wine nights by the fireplace. We transformed her art studio into a vibrant, inspiring space. We started by removing the layer of dust covering the surfaces, bringing in her favorite colors through curtains and decor, and added some pops of blue for creative flow. She sorted through her party serveware and donated or gave away most of the items. We also planned updates for her kids' rooms to shift them from childhood spaces to welcoming adult rooms, hoping to encourage them to visit more often with their spouses.

Carol started to see her home in a new light. It was about letting go of her past and making her space match her present and future.

Sometime later, Carol invited me over to help choose paint colors for the kids' bedrooms. She greeted me with a huge smile. "I can't believe this is the same house," she said. "I feel alive again."

Carol found a way to fall in love with her space all over again, and I couldn't have been happier for her.

CHAPTER 9

Roots Before Wings

NOW THAT YOU'VE HAD A LITTLE SPARK of what juices you up in your home, let's talk about what can ground us and steps to take when life feels like a whirlwind—when the world spins too fast, when we need to slow down and get centered. Maybe you've been practicing yoga or meditation to get grounded but never considered how your surroundings can do the same for you.

TRY THIS ACRONYM FOR GROUNDING: ROOT

R: Reassess Your Space with Fresh Eyes

Take a step back and look at your home with fresh eyes like you're seeing it for the first time. Which areas feel chaotic, cluttered, or stagnant? Ask yourself, "How do these spaces make me feel? Do they align with the energy I want to create?"

Taking some time to intently journal on this can be beneficial. Sit down with a cup of tea and your favorite pen and notebook. Spend ten minutes free writing about your observations and see what comes up. Are there any themes? Is there storage keeping you stuck? Are there inauthentic pieces that don't speak to you? Do any unexpected emotions come up?

O: Organize and Clear Clutter for Calm

Clutter isn't just physical. It can create stress, along with mental and emotional overwhelm. Let go of items that no longer serve you or inspire you. Create organized systems that allow your space to breathe and feel more open, making room for positive energy to flow in. (More on this later in chapter 11.)

O: Optimize Functionality

Ensure your space supports both your daily life and well-being as well as your family's.

Rearrange furniture to encourage more flow, add storage solutions for ease, and make sure each area of your home has a clear purpose. I will forever be a lover of storage ottomans. They're functional yet hide the TV remotes and extra blankets, and they can double as extra seating. Also, a current trend is turning an unused dining room into a functional space such as a lounge, reading room, or game room.

Don't forget an organized mudroom. This is often an overlooked space, but having a place for shoes, schoolbags, and all those other daily needed items can transform the overall function of your home and daily life. A functional home creates a stable foundation for grounding.

T: Tie in Nature for Balance and Peace

Incorporate natural elements like plants, wood, stones, or water features to connect your space to the grounding energy of the earth. These elements calm your mind, create balance, and make the space feel more rooted and serene.

Using ROOT will help you look at various aspects of your home instead of focusing on just one element such as a table or chair. The goal with ROOT is to help you expand your vision to an area or full room and eventually to your entire home.

Take in your space holistically. You'll never look at it the same way again. What are you bringing in? How does it feel? How does it affect your entire home, not just the table it's placed on? Looking at the home holistically rather than in pieces or parts can be the key to creating a space that is supportive during life's challenges.

This brings to mind one of the most impactful experiences in my entire career.

DIANE:
A STORY THAT CHANGED
MY PERSPECTIVE

Diane was a new client who scheduled a consultation without sharing much about her needs. I arrived at her charming brick two-story home, walking up the path lined with beautiful blooming flower beds, carrying my favorite samples and swatches. I felt prepared for just about anything, or so I thought.

When Diane opened the door, she greeted me warmly and invited me inside. Despite her friendliness, I felt an unexplainable heaviness as I crossed the threshold. After a few minutes of small talk, we made our way to the dining table and sat down.

"How can I help you?" I asked gently.

Looking me straight in the eyes, she said, "Lisa, I'm dying. I need your help creating a space so that my husband and children can go on living once I'm gone."

Her words stunned me. My heart raced, and I worked to collect myself. Internally, I was reeling. *Oh, my goodness, I was not expecting that.*

Cancer had been torturing Diane for several years. After enduring countless treatments, the cancer had returned yet again, and she had made the difficult decision to discontinue care. She was tired—physically and emotionally—and wanted to use her remaining time to create a peaceful, nurturing home for her family.

We began discussing her vision for the space which were some basic updates such as new carpeting, fresh furniture, and other small touches to make the home feel complete and comforting. We scheduled a follow-up appointment to review a plan I would create.

As I left her home that day, I felt the weight of her courage and the honor of being trusted with such an important task. This wasn't just about design; it was about creating a legacy of love and comfort that would continue to embrace her family after she was gone.

As I drove home, I couldn't help but think, *Wow, the universe truly connected us for a reason.* This work was clearly my calling. I felt deeply privileged to help Diane create the comforting, healing space she envisioned for her family. Magically, our paths crossed!

The following week, I returned with samples, pricing, and a design plan that Diane completely embraced. We replaced her worn cream carpeting with a cozy, two-tone option, a warm beige with small chocolate flecks to bring grounding energy to the space. Her old sofa and recliner made way for a new, plush sofa paired with two cozy accent chairs. We chose furniture with soft, rounded edges and inviting textures to create a sense of comfort. The beige, tan and brown introduced the earth element of Feng Shui to create grounding.

For accents, we selected plaid pillows in calming blue and green shades to balance the space, and candles of varying heights lit up the unused fireplace, casting a gentle glow. Diane even found a beautiful landscape print tucked away in her closet, rolling hills with a forest, which perfectly brought the essence of nature into the room. We completed the transformation by designing a family photo collage wall that celebrated their cherished vacations, adventures, and memories.

The purpose of this design was multifaceted: to use Feng Shui principles to create balance and grounding, to incorporate natural colors and materials for comfort, to inspire healing through artwork, and to honor the family's journey with a visual celebration of their shared moments. Diane was overjoyed with the results, and I'm grateful she enjoyed this space with her loved ones for nearly two more years.

Working with Diane was life-altering. Her goal in hiring me was to create a space that supported healing and helped her family move forward through difficult times, and I was humbled to help bring that vision to life. Now, whenever I approach a project with a challenging backstory, whether it's illness, loss, or transition, I think of Diane. I remember walking into her home that first day not knowing what lay ahead and the profound beauty of what we created together.

CHAPTER 10

The Truth about Feng Shui: Myths and Facts

WHAT EXACTLY IS FENG SHUI?

Literally translated as "wind and water," Feng Shui is the ancient art and science of arrangement to promote balance in an environment. As I mentioned before, there are various schools or sects that developed from the original Form School, including Compass, BTB and Instinctive, to name a few. Feng Shui is a powerful practice to shift and direct energy for the benefit of the home's occupants. I've been asked more than once if Feng Shui is just superstition. I joke and respond, "No, you can't turn around three times, snap your fingers, and—voila!—your dream home manifests from thin air!"

Now seems like the perfect time to dispel Feng Shui myths. Let's separate fact from fiction.

FENG SHUI: FACT AND FICTION

FICTION: I need to decorate with Asian decor.

Fact: No, not necessarily. There's no need to decorate with Asian decor unless you truly love that look. Implementing Feng Shui does not require you to design in anything other than your preferred style. So, you enjoy rustic, industrial, traditional or ultra-modern? No worries. The best Feng Shui will be felt, not necessarily seen.

FICTION: I need to use the color red throughout.

Fact: Traditionally in Chinese culture red is seen as a color of good luck and prosperity, but if you're not a fan, you don't need to use it.

FICTION: Feng Shui is mostly about furniture arrangement.

Fact: While the arrangement of your furniture can deeply impact the energy of your environment, it's so much more than that. Before you even investigate your home interior, explore what's outside—trees, hills, mountains or sources of water and how your home is positioned among them.

Once we go inside, we look at the floor plan, the room locations, and the flow between spaces. Then it's onto colors, patterns, textures and imagery. This work goes far beyond furniture arrangement.

FICTION: Feng Shui is pricey.

Fact: My favorite projects involved having clients "shop their own home." Look around your space. You probably have some extra taper candles, a colorful throw pillow, or artwork in a basement storage nook. Check to see what you have before you invest. Feng Shui can also be incredibly beneficial when remodeling or even building from scratch. Being able to adjust before the space is finished makes creating that harmonious environment even easier.

FICTION: Feng Shui is a religious practice.

Fact: While Feng Shu has roots in Taoism, it is *not* a religious practice. There's no specific belief system required here. That said, I do ask you to be honest and open to communicating any concerns and wishes. I enjoy working with clients with specific religious beliefs, no matter what that might be. Feng Shui can provide a powerful opportunity to implement beautiful,

HOW FENG SHUI BEGAN

Feng Shui was first recorded more than 4,000 years ago in southern China. It has its roots in Taoist philosophy and is about one central idea: living in harmony with the natural world. In the beginning, practitioners looked closely at the land itself, watching how the mountains, rivers, and even the wind shaped the flow of energy. From there, they chose the most supportive locations initially for burial sites, then homes, and villages, always with the intention of aligning people with the energy around them. Over time, Feng Shui grew into a refined system of principles and patterns, blending observation and symbolism.

sacred symbolism, statues, and artwork in meaningful locations of your home. Additionally, following the Bagua map, we can locate special areas ideal for prayer, yoga, meditation practice, or however you like to reflect and study your belief system.

We'll explore the Bagua Map more closely in Chapter 13.

Feng Shui is less about superstition and more about connection—connection to your home, your surroundings, and yourself.

Once you understand what's myth and what's truth, you can start creating spaces that truly support your life.

CHAPTER 11

Room to Breathe

THE FIRST STEP BEFORE IMPLEMENTING any tweaks in your space is to clear clutter.

I know this is *not* exactly thrilling. People sometimes feel frustrated when they realize they have to clear clutter before we do anything else. They're excited and want to get to the good stuff *now*! But here's what you need to know: The more you tidy, clean, and release what you no longer need, the more powerful your Feng Shu adjustments will be. Slowing down and clearing the clutter is worth it. Trust me!

Clutter clearing isn't just color-coded bins, baskets, and label makers. While I love them galore, this section is about a more spiritual side of clutter. It's about the stories that our stuff tells, the energy that it holds and how it shapes the way we feel about ourselves, our life, others, and even the way we think and move through life.

THE REAL MEANING OF CLUTTER

At its core, clutter is just stuff in limbo— the drawer of unmade decisions, the box in the closet of those "someday" or "just in case" items. Trust me, I've had them. I'm right alongside you. Clutter can also connect to past versions of ourselves that we haven't quite released. Maybe you're doing deep self-development work and trying to be the best version of yourself possible, but something symbolic in your space is holding you back.

I recently attended a four-day retreat hosted by Jill Herman to work on deep inner healing, and when I got home, I realized how the stack of self-development books on my desk sometimes made reading feel like work rather than reading for enjoyment. Keep in mind, the process is not always clearing clutter from your whole home. Sometimes it's the one intentional thing keeping you stuck in the past or with old beliefs. While I often have a stack of one or two books to read, placing them on a bookshelf, and not in a "pile to read" made them feel more special as well as the act of pulling one off the shelf to read more enjoyable.

CLUTTER AND THE SUBCONSCIOUS

Clutter is more than just a mess. Some people have clutter and feel guilty or bad. You may have even been told there's something wrong with you or that you're lazy. Clutter goes deep, though.

Let's first talk about clutter and your subconscious. Every item in your space is there for a reason. It might represent security or safety, maybe a dream or a goal you once had. It might also be tied to someone else's expectations of you. When we look at clutter through our energetic lens, we can see what our clutter is saying, what are we hanging onto, why, and how it might be limiting us?

Years ago, when my husband and I first lived together in St. Louis, we moved to a recently built townhome. We were excited to be in a more centrally located home and embrace the kindness of my in-laws, who came to town to help us move. I'll never forget the expression on my father-in-law's face when he saw my closet and said, "I didn't know someone could have that many clothes!"

I'd never thought twice about my overflowing closet until then. Apparently, I believed, "She who dies with the most clothes wins!" because boy, was I ever overloaded! I didn't realize until years later the depth of what I was doing by keeping all these clothes. The "just-in-case," the maybe "I'll wear-it-again-someday clothes" were hung, stacked and folded. I then started to release clothes, shoes, and accessories I didn't need anymore. I was working and dressing professionally every day and no longer needed some of those clothes left over from my college days.

This effort to pare down continued for many months, some slower than others. In the past few years, I started to take a deeper look and realized just what was happening. I was holding onto clothes as a way of coping, trying to feel safe and fulfilled, making sure I had plenty of options for whatever event was happening. It wasn't just about style or stuff; it was about nervous system regulation.

Once I realized this, I began the practice of releasing even more, starting with clothes and spreading to other areas of my life like keeping my pantry organized and keeping my car tidy. How freeing! I now live with the intention that the item must be worthy to be in my space. It has to be something I love and value, something that brings me joy and is truly deserving of being in my space and my energy field. I now love going to my closet. I don't have to dig through hangers to find my new favorite top; it's right there—front and center—with my other favorite pieces.

THE SPIRITUAL SIDE OF LETTING GO

Having a clutter-free home isn't just about being tidy. I've seen some immaculate, organized homes filled with so many unnecessary items. It's about honoring flow, a sense of freedom, and being open to the next chapter of your life—perhaps a new job, new relationship, or even new hobbies. When our homes are filled with stuck, stagnant energy, we can feel like someone hit the pause button on our lives. I've been there; it can feel tough. Letting go isn't just a physical act but a spiritual and emotional one. The process says, "I'm ready for my next chapter. I'm making space for what's next."

I also release and make space in my office with my file folders. While I have most of my client information on my computer, I still keep a paper file. Sometimes I'll doodle, have a swatch or sample, or just want to keep a handwritten note. Whenever I tie up a project with a client, I take their paper file, hold it in my hands, and give it love and gratitude. I then file it away and immediately afterward pull out a fresh new file ready for the next client. And just like clockwork, a new client appears! Maybe I'm old school or just love the energetic experience here. Either way, it works.

"JUST IN CASE" IS FEAR IN DISGUISE

Let's approach those all-important "just-in-case" items, those "someday" items or the "what if I need it again" items. These items are code for, "What if I'm not supported in the future?" This question represents a sense of lacking or a sense of fear. When we hold onto that sense of fear, we block the flow of energy. It's like hitting the brakes, gripping, hanging on.

Maybe you have the old jeans you want to fit into "someday" or the drawer of old cords to random cell phones. Everything in your home affects the Feng Shui. It leans into a positive space or negative space. It reinforces scarcity or abundance. Your choice.

A RITUAL FOR RELEASING WITH INTENTION

Remember Marie Kondo? She asked you to see if things sparked joy. While I want you to find joy in your home, we're not doing that here. We're connecting to things on a deep level.

1. Start by scheduling this ritual with intention; add it in your calendar tonight, tomorrow, or for this weekend.

2. Wear something you love like your favorite top or some colorful sneakers that bring you joy.

3. Choose some inspirational music and light a candle.

4. Choose one corner of your home.

5. Pick up each item. Hold it in your hands and ask, "Does this represent who I'm becoming?" Yes or no?

If the answer is no, it's time to release it. Donate, gift, recycle, or throw it in the trash bin.

This is not decluttering; this is a ceremony to connect with the items in your home. All you need to do is one small corner, one section at a time.

As you move throughout this corner, remember to move with intention and with presence. You're not clutter clearing or sparking joy; you're experiencing a beautiful moment to connect with your space.

Find your next corner next weekend. This will bring lighter, better energy to the entire space. You might feel like you can breathe easier or the energy feels different. Maybe you feel more present in your space.

Let this section be an invitation to look deeper, an invitation to dig deeper yet remember that clutter is not the enemy. Clutter is a mirror, a teacher as well as a beautiful opportunity.

Maybe you've concluded that you truly have excess like I did in my closet, what's next? No fear, my friend! Keep reading.

MOST COMMON TYPES OF CLUTTER I SEE IN HOMES

- Items you don't use
- Housewares that are broken or don't function
- Anything you don't love
- Unwanted gifts
- Old cleaning and care products
- Old, worn-out clothing and shoes
- Books you don't read and magazines that are outdated
- Extra electrical cords and chargers

Clutter can bring on a lot of emotions, and sorting through clutter can feel like an overwhelming mountain to climb, so get the help that you need. In every city, expert organizations, amazing clutter coaches, and home organizers are thoroughly trained to help you navigate your "stuff" *and* your emotions. Don't forget to work with your therapist for extra help in clutter clearing too.

MY TIPS FOR CLUTTER CLEARING

1. Put Together a Plan
Decide how you'll work: top to bottom, left to right, or clockwise.

2. Develop and Document
Write down all the tasks needed and how you'll achieve each step. The more you can detail in an outline, spreadsheet or list, or even color coding, the better.

3. Gather Supplies
Gather boxes, bins, labels, markers, scissors and garbage bags before you start.

4. Sort
Set up a sorting system with bins labeled "Donation," "Landfill," "Toss," "Giveaway," "Shred," and "Keep."

Looking for more? I've got you, check out the "pro tips" on the next page.

Pro Tips

1. Never begin with any sentimental items

They can bring on the most emotion, so start with the linen closet or junk drawer. Starting with these easier, less emotion-filled spaces can also help you cultivate a sense of accomplishment that propels you forward with a feeling of encouragement.

I always begin decluttering with the linen closet. Somehow, I've developed a knack for keeping bath towels and washcloths way too long. I eventually realized what I was doing. I now either transition them to the "dog towel" pile or donate them to the local animal shelter.

—Lisa

2. Set the energy you wish to create

Get up on time and get dressed. Change out of your pajamas and put on something that feels good. Maybe your favorite pair of jeans and graphic tee with a positive message. Pop your hair in a ponytail and sip on some coffee. When you're ready, turn on some music. Play something that you can dance or sing to while cleaning. I love to listen to an 80's/90's playlist and sing along to my favorite songs. Opt for diffusing some aromatherapy too. I love a citrus scent, particularly sweet orange in my diffuser when I'm cleaning or clutter clearing.

Don't forget to get some fresh air while you're working. Crack open the window for even a few moments to allow some fresh air to blow.

> Remember to take breaks when needed. Take a walk outside and have a nourishing snack. My favorite pick-me-up snack is an apple and peanut butter, or I might have a handful of nuts and dried fruit.
>
> —*Lisa*

3. Ask for Support

Ask a friend to check on you during the day. Maybe a family member can swing by and bring lunch or schedule a pre-clutter clearing appointment with your therapist to discuss strategies for handling items with heavy energy and emotions attached.

> Keeping a journal and pen on hand can help with feeling overwhelmed if you don't have anyone to talk to.
> Write out all your feelings whether they're in sentence form, bullet points or just scribbles. Just get it out!
>
> —*Lisa*

TIMEFRAMES TO DECLUTTER

While I love to recommend taking time over a weekend to clear out clutter. There are two other approaches to consider.

If you can't devote a day or weekend, devote ten minutes a day every day for a week. Maybe a five-minute clutter-clearing session twice a day is all you can do. That's ok. Remember, the more you do, the better the overall outcome, but be realistic. Set yourself up for success, not frustration or guilt.

Sometimes, it's not clearing your entire home of clutter but rather one intentional space that needs to be done. A single box was deterring my client, Angela, from ever going into her basement. This box was filled with paperwork left to her after her parents had passed away. She dreaded ever having to go through it. It was easier to place the box in the basement and not have to look at it. Sure, she didn't have to walk past it daily with it being in the basement, but it was still subconsciously cueing stress.

When we talked about it further, she said that she'd even felt guilty when she simply glanced at the basement door. She had shared with me clear goals of moving into a new home and moving forward with other aspects of her life, but this box was standing in her way, and she knew it. I recommended some support from her therapist as she went through this box, and that helped. She even said it wasn't as difficult as she'd expected, and the process even felt a bit healing. The bonus is she's now living in her brand-new home ready for some new opportunities.

THE SYMBOLIC POWER OF CLUTTER

According to the National Association of Professional Organizers (NAPO), 80% of what we keep is never used.[5] Ever! You're certainly not going to use something by shoving it into the back of a closet! Remember earlier when I mentioned how you subconsciously continue to respond to items even though your conscious mind doesn't recognize it? That box of paperwork shoved in a corner is still affecting you.

Get this: The brain can't tell the difference between reality and symbolism. This can work against us or for us. If you constantly feel less than, not worthy of having a space that feels good or inspires you, you're reiterating that message to yourself. Old, worn-out furniture that says, "I'm not deserving," empty walls that say, "Who cares?" tells you you're not good enough. Clutter everywhere says, "I feel less than."

REMEMBER

The brain can't tell the difference between reality and symbolism, which means that the mind responds to both in very similar ways. For example, when you walk into a cluttered and messy room, your nervous system can register it as stress. Even though the "threat" isn't real danger, your body reacts as if it is. On the flip side, when you place a symbol of something you desire like a vision board image of a peaceful yoga retreat or a bowl of fresh fruit to represent health, your brain interprets it as if you're already experiencing that reality.

This is why Feng Shui and intentional design are so powerful. The objects, colors, and symbols you surround yourself with aren't just décor; they're sending constant messages to your subconscious.

---

5   Martha Spittal, "80/20 Your 2018," NAPO, Dec 26, 2017, https://www.napo-gpc.org/8020-your-2018/.

On the flip side, it can also work for you. If your brain thinks you have a red convertible in the garage, then certainly you must. Before you know it, it can be true. If your office displays your certificates and awards that you're proud of, then you're implementing the energy that you're a success and ready for more. So, before we go further, put together a plan to take on some clutter or cleaning and get things in order.

One item, one corner, one release at a time. You decide.

CHAPTER 12

The Heart of Feng Shui

So, you've cleared the clutter, made space to breathe. Now, my friend, it's time to step into the heart of Feng Shui.

YING AND YANG

Feng Shui is all about balance, just like the black and white yin/yang symbol that you may have seen. Anyone else have a yin/yang necklace back in the 90s? Yin and Yang represent the interconnectedness of opposites in the natural world. The design represents how they complement and balance each other.

Yin is associated with qualities like darkness, femininity, and receptivity, while yang represents light, masculinity, and action. Together, they illustrate the harmony of duality, reminding us that one cannot exist without the other. We can't have light without dark, daytime without nighttime, loud without quiet. In Feng Shui, we work to create balance between yin and yang while keeping in mind the activity happening in the space.

Think about the last time you were at a quiet, cozy coffee shop—so peaceful with soft music, warm drinks, and ambient lighting. The energy here is meant to be slightly more yin than yang, more restful than active.

Now think of the last time you were at a big box store. The energy here is meant to lean more yang—crowds, loud music, bright lights, a commotion of people, and everything giant sized!

THE FIVE ELEMENTS: NATURE'S ENERGY IN MOTION

The five elements—Wood, Fire, Earth, Metal and Water—are the foundation of Feng Shui. They describe how energy flows and can be a tool to adjust the flow in an environment.

Here's how the elements flow:

- Wood energy is strong and moving upward.
- Fire energy is exciting and bold.
- Earth energy is grounded and stable.
- Metal energy is focused and intentional.
- Water energy is relaxed and fluid.

HOW TO BRING THE ELEMENTS INTO YOUR HOME

Wood

The wood element is about healing, growth and vitality.

Bring it in through the color of green, vertical stripes, or vertical elements such as columns and detailed trim work. Any wood furniture or flooring works well. Consider plants and flowers, including artwork depicting plants and flowers. Large scale floral wallpaper is experiencing a comeback in interior design, so consider selecting a bold floral for your next bathroom remodel.

> **Quick scan:** Do you see any examples
> of a wood element in your space?

Fire

This yang energy element can sometimes feel like the most impactful because fire packs a punch. It brings the essence of passion, success, boldness, and transformation. When fire is missing, a space can feel sleepy. Introduce this element through the colors of red, fuchsia or purple. Triangular shapes, animal prints, fur or faux fur, or artwork depicting animal or animal prints are great. Don't forget candles and lighting. I recently worked with a client where we found a stunning triangular patterned fabric that we used for throw pillows. A few small throw pillows can alter the whole space on a budget.

> **Quick scan:** Do you see any Fire element?

Earth

Most homes can benefit from more of the earth element. Our lives are go-go, and we're constantly trying to keep up. When you feel like a paper bag floating in the wind, you need the earth element to inspire a more grounded feeling and set yourself up to be more calm and centered. Bring in the colors of beige, tan, brown and yellow. Also, opt for square shapes and lower linear furniture pieces such as sofas and coffee tables. Look for rocks, crystals, ceramic, or clay pottery. Those days when I feel I can't keep up with my schedule, I'll even dress in earth element colors to stay grounded.

Quick scan: Any Earth element in sight?

Metal

Metal has an essence of precision, focus, and productivity, so we often think about using it in office spaces, but every space should offer some metal element energy for balancing free-flowing elements and introducing structure into an environment.

Bring in metal objects such as lamps and overhead light fixtures made of metal, accent tables and shelving. You can also invite it in through gray, white and pastel colors. Circular shapes bring in this element, so opt for the round cabinet pulls versus square or rectangular shape.

I recently helped a client add some round metal end tables into a sitting room for balance. They were the perfect touch of interest and function, plus they brought in the needed metal into the room to balance the other soft, textural and earthy furniture.

Quick scan: Do you see Metal elements?

Water

Water, which is more yin in energy, brings in a sense of fluidity, allowing for inspiration, creativity, and abundance. Water and blue are my favorites.

By adding more water, you may feel that you can go with the flow and daydream a bit. Use blue and black colors, wavy patterns or designs and images or artwork of water. Or consider fish tanks and water features.

Quick scan: Any water flowing through?

Feeling the Balance

When I first started with Feng Shui, I got overwhelmed with balancing each element "just right." Now, after working with it for many years, I'm able to feel it even before I look deeper at the items in the space. I can sense the instant I walk in a room if it's out of balance and needs more fire, water, or maybe earth. Eventually, you may find yourself feeling this way too. However, if you're looking around your space feeling overwhelmed, try this:

> Close your eyes, take a few deep breaths, then open them with the intention of seeing your space with fresh perspective. (This is similar to the "front door" experiment we did earlier.) What elements do you see? Name them or write them down. Then take inventory and notice what could be introduced for more balance. A few silver candle holders for metal? Maybe a rectangular shaped rug on the floor in a cozy brown texture for earth. Maybe some wall art with vertical stripes.

Please remember, perfectionism is *not* your friend. So often, my students want the exact balance of each element down to a calculated number, just as I did when I started. As I previously mentioned though, consider the use of the space. How can you balance the elements for the actual activity in the space? Instead of counting the elements and creating a spreadsheet in your head, think of yin/yang on a sliding scale. A spa requires an environment that leans more yin in energy. You walk in and hear soft soothing music, sense the muted colors, dimmed lighting, and a soft, textural robe. A more active space such as a gym requires more energy to ensure you have a feeling of lifted energy and keep moving on the treadmill. When you're looking to balance the five elements, be sure the custom balance of elements enhances the energy of a space. Chuck E. Cheese sure would be boring for little ones if it had beige carpeting, no music, and silent games!

ALISON'S DINING ROOM MAKEOVER

Allison needed help transforming her dining room. She loved hosting her friends for dinner parties because she loved to cook, but there was a problem. Whenever it was her turn to host the group, the energy of the evening just fell flat. Conversations were minimal, and the room felt, as she described it, "sleepy and boring." It wasn't anything like the lively, fun gatherings they enjoyed at other friends' homes.

Her dining room was stunning, with elegant white marble floors and a gorgeous chandelier. Yet, despite its beauty, the room didn't feel right. Allison couldn't put her finger on it, but she knew something about the mood of the space wasn't working.

As soon as I walked in, I felt it. The room was visually beautiful but energetically cold. The marble floors, paired with gray walls and solid, hard materials, lacked warmth and vibrancy. The abundance of gray was bringing in the metal element, an effective choice for focus and clarity but not for fostering free-flowing, joyful and fun conversation. The oval shape of the room, while unique, also presented a challenge: It amplified the echo, making the acoustics feel harsh and uninviting.

HERE'S WHAT WE DID:

- Layered in elements that softened the space and the energy. We chose a blue patterned fabric for her dining chair cushions to bring in the water element, which promotes flow and connection.

- Hung colorful artwork to liven up the walls

- Replaced her boxy rectangular dining table with an oval one that worked beautifully with the shape of the room. This oval shape reduced the angular energy.

- Addressed the acoustics. We added curtain panels in a beautiful floral pattern with a sound-absorbing backing, which helped soften the echo while adding visual texture and warmth.

- Placed a plush area rug under the table, further absorbing sound and bringing about a sense of grounding.

- Brought in fresh flowers that added a nice touch of nature and the wood element.

REMEMBER

The Five Elements

Wood

Fire

Earth

Metal

Water

When the next dinner party rolled around, Allison was ready and excited. The new design created a cozy, vibrant atmosphere where people felt comfortable and energized. This time, the room was buzzing with laughter and engaging conversations. She called me afterward, thrilled to report that the night was a hit, and for the first time, her dining room was truly a reflection of the warm, welcoming host she wanted to be. Her friends were already asking when her next party was going to be!

Feng Shui isn't about perfection. It's about creating a space that feels alive. When yin and yang are in harmony and the five elements are balanced, the whole room shifts. Play with it, trust your instincts, and watch how small changes spark big transformations in your home and in your life.

CHAPTER 13

Mapping Your Home's Hidden Energy

THE BAGUA MAP IS A VISUAL TOOL that shows how your home connects to different aspects of your life and highlights where you can make changes to create more harmony. It helps you understand the energy flow of your space by dividing it into nine key energy centers.

Included in this map are energy centers connected to the following:

- Knowledge and Self-Cultivation
- Career and Lifepath
- Helpful People and Travel
- Family and Ancestors
- Health

- Children and Creativity
- Wealth and Abundance
- Fame and Reputation
- Love and Relationships

I encourage my clients and students to make a list of these nine areas and journal about each one. Be specific and write down as much as you'd like. You might even take a few days to write and journal on each area.

Ask yourself:

1. What's going well?
2. What's not going well?
3. How would you like things to shift?

Now that you know which areas you need to address, let's understand where those energy centers are in your home.

MAPPING THE BAGUA

First, find your home's architectural or builder's drawings or create your own floorplan sketch. Be sure to note the exterior and interior walls, doors and windows and be sure to locate the front entry. If you're creating a sketch, it doesn't have to be drawn to-scale. but try to make it somewhat proportional.

You can apply the Bagua Map in a few ways depending on your hemisphere and the Feng Shui school you're using. I use the Three Gate Method for applying the Bagua, which was created by Professor

Thomas Lin Yun, who recognized that our energies, thoughts, perceptions, and values hold the greatest influence over our lives and the environments we are looking to create. This means our personal energies flow into our spaces and shape the energetic patterns within them.

HERE'S HOW TO APPLY THE BAGUA:

1. Line up the bottom of the map with your front door.

2. Your front door will likely be in one of the three boxes at the bottom (Knowledge and Self Cultivation, Career and Lifepath, or Helpful People and Travel).

3. Map out the rest of your entire home. From the front door, I like to move left to Knowledge and Self Cultivation and then continue circling around.

4. Use colored markers or highlighters to note on your floorplan so you have a quick reference.

5. Not every home is a perfect square, so do your best. Focus on the front door, the center, and then build off those areas lining up the longest walls of your home with the map.

6. You may find that there are areas missing. Fortunately, there are Feng Shui adjustments to energetically extend the energy beyond the structure using symbolism. My favorite way to incorporate this is by using rocks and crystals.

WEALTH AND ABUNDANCE	FAME AND REPUTATION	LOVE AND RELATIONSHIPS
Wood Element	*Fire Element*	*Earht Element*
Purple, Green, Blue, and Red	Red	Pink, White, and Brown
FAMILY AND ANCESTORS	HEALTH	CHILDREN AND CREATIVITY
Wood Element	*Earth Element*	*Metal Element*
Green and Blue	Yellow, Orange, and Brown	White and Pastels
KNOWLEDGE AND SELF CULTIVATION	CAREER	HELPFUL PEOPLE AND TRAVEL
Earth Element	*Water Element*	*Metal Element*
Blue, Green, and Brown	Blue and Black	Gray, White, and Pastels

BRING THE BAGUA TO LIFE

You've got your floorplan applied, so how in the world do you begin to enhance an area?

Here's an example: Say you're looking to cultivate more self-love. Once you've located that love and relationships area, bring in some items that remind you to care for yourself. Maybe a luxurious pink robe, a rose quartz stone or a red candle in the Love & Relationships area.

CHRISTINA'S STORY

Christina wanted to improve the finances of her retail jewelry store. We located the Wealth & Abundance energy center and added a bamboo plant for a wood element, some Chinese coins for wealth, and purple wall art (her favorite color and a wealth symbol). Even with these simple adjustments, she had an uptick in sales and made huge strides in growing her business. She also took on a successful local jewelry artist, which caused some excitement in her community.

ANDY'S STORY

Andy and his wife were desperate for better health. He'd been grappling with his recent weight gain, and they were both having trouble finding time to exercise. Their daughter was constantly fighting a bug, and the family cat was sick. The Bagua showed that their Health area was cluttered, especially their hall closet. We decluttered, donated old coats, recycled school papers (with their daughter's approval), and organized extra hats and gloves. We also added some fresh flowers and a new houseplant on the shelf nearby.

We then put a plan in place to keep the closet as tidy as possible. We added bins and baskets to keep like items together, arranged the remaining coats nicely, and Andy agreed to my "one in, one out" method. Every time he'd bring in a new item such as a winter hat or a pair of gloves, a pair had to be donated.

The overflowing mess and disorganization in this closet and area of the home was mimicking their bodies and health. Once we cleared the physical mess, vitality could flow again, and the family's health vastly improved.

TWO QUICK ADJUSTMENTS YOU CAN MAKE TODAY

Many people enjoy working with the Bagua and feel like it's an easy reference. Once they can understand their layout, they feel like they have a clearer direction to making life easier. If the Bagua is feeling too much for you though, here are two of my favorite, easy-to-implement adjustments.

THE COMMAND POSITION

One of the most impactful tools of Feng Shui whenever I'm stressed is the placement of the Command Position. The ancients recommended a mountain behind the home for protection and an open valley below so that you could see any enemies approaching. In modern times, this is where you have a solid supportive wall behind you yet can see anything in front of you. This is called the Command Position.

Place your bed in the command position for restful sleep. Your bed should be against a solid wall, and you should have a clear view of the entry door off to one side. A solid headboard preferably made of wood or upholstery is ideal.

In your home office, avoid having your back exposed. Instead, have a wall behind you and again, a view of the door.

I even use this when going out to eat at a restaurant. If I'm tired from a long week and not feeling my best, I'll ask for the table with a solid wall behind. Have an important presentation to a high-profile client? Opt for the solid wall, not windows or an open walkway behind you while presenting. Not only will their energy be focused more on you, but you'll feel more supported and confident.

WATCH FOR POISON ARROWS

Feeling like you just can't relax? Poison arrows in Feng Shui may just be the culprit.

Poison arrows are created by sharp angles, corners, or structures that point directly at you. They can bring feelings of discomfort, anxiety, tension, and even block positive energy flow. You may not even realize this is the cause of your discomfort until you look around.

EXAMPLES:

Sharp Corners

Imagine a sharp corner of a buffet pointing directly at you. It sends a subconscious signal to your body that something is "off." You might notice that it feels harder to relax and enjoy your dinner.

Maybe a corner of a coffee table or a bookend with a sharp point is directed at you. Can you feel it? When shopping for furniture and décor, look for more curved and rounded designs.

Spiky Plants - Sorry, desert lovers

The sharp points of cacti or yuca don't inspire you to rest and relax. Instead, opt for plants with soft, rounded leaves such as a jade or fern.

While it can be hard to avoid poison arrows all the time, be mindful of how long you're exposed to a poison arrow. Think of these areas where you spend long periods of time and start there. Make sure your bed and perhaps your desk position avoids poison arrows if possible.

Solutions

- Hang a cut glass prism to disperse harsh energy.
- Rearrange furniture to avoid direct aim.
- Use rounded shapes to soften the effects.

The Bagua isn't simply a Feng Shui tool. It's a roadmap for living with more intention. Whether you fully map your entire home or start with a few simple adjustments, you're taking powerful steps toward aligning your environment with the life you want to create.

CHAPTER 14

Trusting the Inner Compass

WHEN MOST PEOPLE HEAR Feng Shui, they think of rules.

Do this.

Don't do that.

Move this over here.

Never put that over there.

I recently had a discussion with some yoga friends. We were chatting casually, and my work came up. "Oh, I don't have good Feng Shui in my home at all!" Another agreed and said she didn't have good Feng Shui either.

I'd never been in either of their homes, but I know this: They're some positive women full of life and vibrancy who often share stories about family gatherings or celebrations in their home and how much they enjoy them.

I asked them, "Do you love your home?" They both gave me a solid yes.

I happily responded, "Then I'd say you already have good Feng Shui."

They were thinking of Feng Shui as simply good or bad, right or wrong. They were also stuck on the fact that they have clutter. Here's the thing. Nearly everyone has some sort of clutter. We just need to be mindful of clutter and do what we can. Instead of getting hung up on perfect arrangement and location and clutter, do this:

THE SLIDING SCALE

Think of your space on a sliding scale. Not good or bad, but where is it currently on a scale?

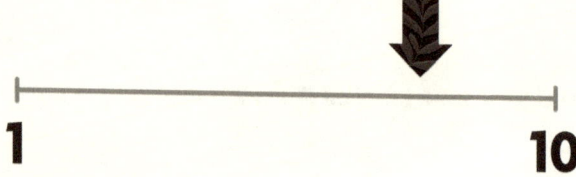

- Number 1: Your home doesn't feel supportive in any way. Life feels difficult. You're overwhelmed with more than you feel you can handle.

- Number 10: You feel vibrant and healthy, your relationships are solid, your day-to-day flows, and you're a happy camper.

Where's your home on this scale right now?

It's natural for us to hear about Feng Shui and diagnose or decipher each item and determine whether it's good or bad. The problem is we become overwhelmed and can lose the joy of turning a house into a supportive home. What starts as the excitement of filling your space with things that bring happiness can quickly shift into the stress of constantly arranging and redesigning it. You begin to question everything and where you're placing it.

ENTER: INSTINCTIVE FENG SHUI™

This is where Instinctive Feng Shui™ comes in. It allows you to take a breath and really feel deep into your body and soul and ask, "What do I need?" Denise Linn coined this term "Instinctive" Feng Shui because we need to listen to our core intuition.

Feng Shui's rules and practices have been around for centuries, and it works. But sometimes you need to take a dose of that information and explore how it feels to you. Linn believes that "the answers to our deepest questions are held inside the subconscious mind."

By asking the right questions and taking part in deep guided visualization, I can help a client uncover their deepest desire, even if they didn't realize it.

TRUST THE VOICE

You know that feeling that you can't shake, the thought or concern keeps popping in your head? Maybe you have that sensation deep in the pit of your stomach.

The next time this happens, try this:

- Ask that feeling, "What do you have to tell me?"

- Then just listen. This can be hard. Be patient and listen.

- Nothing coming up? Grab a notebook and free-write. Set a timer for ten minutes and just write anything that comes up about the feeling you're grappling with.

Now I know you might be jumping to grab your phone or type on your computer, but I strongly encourage you to put pen to paper. Handwriting words on a page can be transformative. In fact, some of the free-writing I did prior to this book helped determine the direction of the book, and if you read the introduction, you know it's not the book I planned to write.

A WALK THROUGH YOUR HOME AS YOU

It's time to apply that understanding to your own space. Remember the earlier exercise where you entered your home as a stranger? This time, walk in as yourself. Move slowly—what catches your eye? How does your body respond? Notice if a piece of art lifts your energy or weighs it down. Pick up objects and feel their effect.

FINDING YOUR DEEPER CONNECTION

The best way to get connected and "see" or "hear" what your home is telling you is to slow down. I have two favorite activities that inspire me to be open and aware: The first is journaling, the second is meditation. Now before you start thinking, *No way can I meditate,* let me explain.

JOURNALING

Journaling is a beautiful practice that can help you with mindfulness and intuition. There's no right or wrong way.

You may:

- Use a daily prompt, such as "I'm grateful for" or "Thoughts from the day."

- Free-write whatever comes to mind, using a pen or pencil and paper. (Yes, even "I had salad for dinner" counts.) You might find something profound finds its way onto your page.

I've found free writing challenging because my hand doesn't write with a pen as fast as I can type, but during a workshop with my writing coach, Gail, something shifted. On Day 1, I thought, *This is going to be frustrating,* but after my hand slowed down to actually write something legible, my brain slowed down and beautiful words began to fill my page.

If you're like me—a fast talker and a fast thinker who has troubled writing with a pen and paper, I have two tips for you:

1. Get a beautiful pen and beautiful journal you love

Make sure the pen fits between your fingers perfectly and scrolls on the page just the way you like. Then your journal can be spiral or hardbound. Make sure you love the beautiful image or the inspirational quote on the front.

2. Play music

Calming sounds can quiet the mind.

> I find my favorite journals at bookstores and craft stores and love a gel pen. My favorite journaling music is a Spotify playlist called *Healing and Cleansing Frequencies.*
>
> —*Lisa*

MEDITATION

I've practiced meditation off and on for almost fifteen years. Sometimes, I'll go months without missing a day; other times, I can't sit still for more than three minutes and then skip two weeks.

One book that helped me transform my meditation practice is *Meditation for Fidgety Skeptics* by Dan Harris. Harris was an ABC news anchor who had a panic attack live on the air. (yes, you can google it). He wasn't living a healthy lifestyle, and this was his tipping point. In his healing journey, he found meditation as his answer. While he now meditates for multiple hours every day, the approach he lays out is quite simple and refreshing. He encourages you to simply start with sixty seconds. If you're fidgety or think meditation is just for "crunchy people doing pretzel-ish yoga," then you are in for a treat.

I used to have an internal fight with my twenty-minute timer. I'd start, and after what felt like an eternity, I'd peek at the clock to realize it had only been three whole minutes. After reading Harris' book, I decided to start devoting whatever time I could. Of course, the more frazzled you feel, the more time you should try to devote to your practice, but do what you can. Can you do three minutes today? Great. Thirty minutes the next day? Fantastic! Just the act of sitting down to do it is significant.

CREATE A MEDITATION STATION

Your space may be a quiet room or maybe just your favorite chair in the corner. I've also designed several meditation rooms, and many have been spare walk-in closets! Have a cozy blanket, a table for a cup of tea, maybe a candle or aromatherapy diffuser. Set the stage for success. The more you commit to getting yourself to your Meditation Station each day, the more comfortable it will be and eventually more meaningful. Now, I simply crave my meditation time. I look forward to it every day just as much as I do when I open my door at the end of the day and have my dogs joyfully greet me.

A FINAL NOTE ON MEDITATION

Remember, each time you're just sitting down or bringing your attention back to your breath during a session, you're recommitting. You're taking a moment to prioritize and saying yes to this practice instead of giving up.

I'm proud of you. Know that every time you bring your attention back to your breath during a session and let go of your afternoon errands, I'm there in the background cheering you on.

CHAPTER 15

Awakening the Five Senses

COLOR YOUR WORLD

Color is often the first element you notice when entering a room. Your eyes might catch the blond wood floors, white painted cabinetry, or the red sofa. We're drawn to color because it helps us easily distinguish one item from another. But did you know color isn't tangible? It's how we perceive light. This helps us navigate and understand our spaces.

Color can also be a powerful tool for influencing the energy of a room and your body. Stressed out from a busy job? Use peaceful and calming pale blue and soft green. Need to lift your energy during the cold, dreary days of late winter? Cheerful colors like yellow, orange and pink are the answer.

Color psychology studies show how colors affect mood and behavior. Common knowledge says that cool colors bring a sense of calm, and warm colors lift our energy, but it goes much beyond that. People may react to colors differently depending on their nervous system. In my bi-monthly online Color Mastery course, we explore this deeply.

I recall when I had difficulty sleeping and had a red upholstered headboard. What's wrong with a red upholstered headboard, you ask? If only I knew then what I know now. Red, which leans more yang, can prevent you from finding restful sleep and cause you to toss and turn all night because red keeps your energy level lifted too high for rest.

Let's check out some popular colors and their effects on your body, emotions, and mood.

YELLOW—BOOST YOUR MOOD

Yellow is the color of sunshine and joy. In Feng Shui, this color connects to the earth element yet is more high energy than beige or tan. Perfect for kitchens and living rooms where you want to feel energized and joyful. You might also consider a soft yellow in an office if you need help with focus.

BLUE—FIND PEACE AND FLOW

Blue is known to promote peace, calm, and rest. Using shades of blue in bedrooms creates a serene and relaxing environment. I also love to bring some blue into a creative or artistic area because it connects to the water element of Feng Shui and inspires fluidity and creativity.

PURPLE—CREATE LUXURY AND MAGIC

Purple embodies luxury and royalty. It also has a magical and mystical vibe and was the key ingredient to one of my favorite yoga studio projects. With a soft purple on the walls and candles lit, the evening yoga classes were wondrous.

GREEN—INVITE IN HARMONY

Green symbolizes nature and renewal, creating a sense of balance and harmony. It's especially effective in living rooms and home offices, bringing in the wood element.

BROWN—BECOME GROUNDED

You know that feeling of running around feeling frazzled? Brown is your friend. Brown evokes feelings of stability and reliability. Incorporate brown tones in furniture and decor to create a grounded and nourishing space. You'll instantly be able to feel your feet on the ground and shoulders drop being surrounded by the color brown because it's an earth element of Feng Shui.

WHITE AND GRAY—ENHANCE FOCUS

While white represents purity and cleanliness, gray inspires focus and precision. Both introduce the metal element of Feng Shui. Bring these colors into your workspace to create focus and productivity. I recommend a metal desk lamp or metal desk accessories. Have a deadline quickly approaching? I suggest wearing some gray for added precision and focus.

ORANGE—SPARK JOY

Many don't think of using orange, but it's a vibrant, energetic color that, like yellow, can spark joy and creativity but at a higher energy level than yellow. Perfect for social areas like dining rooms and family rooms where you want to encourage lively conversations, fun, and warmth. It's one of my favorite colors for a workout room. If you've ever been to Orange Theory for a workout class, you'll remember that orange glow in their fitness studio that keeps your energy high for the whole workout.

RED—ENERGIZE, BUT WITH CARE

Red is a passionate, powerful color that can stimulate energy and passion but also your blood pressure. Use it sparingly if you or your family members struggle with stress or anxiety. I do recommend it, though, for exercise rooms to boost motivation and drive. And red inspires passion, so try a pair of small red candles in the bedroom.

BEFORE YOU COMMIT

Test, test, test! Before committing to a color, take the time to explore it in your space. If you're feeling uncertain, try incorporating the color through smaller accents first. For example, if you're considering a beautiful teal, start by adding a few throw pillows, a candle, or other decorative items in that shade. This allows you to experience the color before making a bigger commitment, like painting a wall. Spend some time with these colors.

One client was set on painting her living room aqua blue. Her home, however, was filled with heavy, ornate décor and deep browns—making aqua a poor fit. Instead of painting, I suggested she test the color with inexpensive accessories like a throw and pillows. A week later, she called to say the color felt wrong the moment she unpacked it. We chose a lighter beige for the walls to keep things cozy yet bright, and I encouraged her to enjoy aqua in her wardrobe instead.

THE POWER OF SCENT

We see color and we've discussed how it impacts our emotions, behavior and mood, but smells can also have a transformative effect.

Do you have a favorite childhood smell? Mine is my mom's meatloaf in the oven that made my mouth water and brought me joy knowing I'd have one of my favorite comfort foods. I also loved the smell of the lilac bush blooming in the spring. While the scent didn't last very long, it was a sign that summer was soon on its way. I associated that smell with the timing of summer break from school and couldn't have been more excited.

This is a perfect example of the **Proustian Memory Effect**, a term inspired by French writer Marcel Proust. He described how a specific scent or taste can unlock vivid memories. In his case, it happened while eating a madeleine soaked in tea. The aroma and flavor instantly brought back memories of enjoying the same treat with his aunt, which then led to a flood of other childhood memories.

Maybe you've been to the beautiful hotel chain where they pump in the luxurious scent throughout the HVAC system, the retail store that has that familiar smell, or your favorite spa with its relaxing eucalyptus scents. "Scent branding" or "olfactory branding" has become an integral part of business alongside logos and color palettes. I even jumped on this idea years back.

A real estate office I had previously designed reached out about constant bickering between agents. Could I work my "woo magic" on the space?

The design wasn't the problem—the heavy energy was. Since smudging with sage wasn't allowed, I created my **Good Chi Space Clearing Spritz**. I'd long used essential oils and water to refresh spaces, but I wanted a tool clients could use anytime as both a reset and a gentle reminder. The oils from plants with the transformative power of water is just the ticket to reset an environment. With just a couple spritzes, they could be transformed back to their zone of comfort, positivity, and clarity. The real estate office used this spritz daily to reset the energy of the office, and the entire staff found more peace and calm too. They even began to refer to it as the "magical scent."

TUNE IN, SHIFT YOUR MOOD

Music is another powerful tool that we can bring into the home, and it's not just about creating a vibe. Music can shift emotions. Research shows that music lights up some of the most widespread and diverse areas of the brain. Sure, it starts in the auditory cortex which is the part of the brain that processes sound, but it doesn't stop there. Emotional music syncs up the parts of the brain that process feelings, which is why we can be moved to tears by a certain favorite song or feel uplifted by another.

A few years ago, I traveled to Charleston where I attended a workshop by Meadow Linn, Denise Linn's creative and artistic daughter. In the writing portion of the workshop, we explored our writing with various genres of music. We experimented with listening to jazz while we wrote for ten minutes, then rock for ten minutes, relaxing guitar for ten minutes, and so on. It was wild just how different my writing was as she played the various types of music. I was having a direct response to what I was hearing, and it was coming out through the words on the page.

I have a playlist for when I've had a long day and am feeling a bit down. You'll hear a variety of The Rolling Stones, Taylor Swift, Fleetwood Mac, and even Bill Wither's "Lovely Day." My husband has his favorite driving song, the memorable, "In the Air Tonight" by Phil Collins. He plays it as loud as the volume will go!

What's your song? This is your cue to create a playlist.

CREATING A VIBE WITH SOUND

Music allows us to infuse our spaces with the energy of a particular sound. Specific frequencies of sound are particularly healing to our bodies and our environment. For example, 40 Hz supports focus and cognitive function, while 432 Hz brings balance and a sense of emotional wellbeing. Confused? Head over to Spotify and search for various Hz. Play it throughout your home to infuse it with that frequency.

Various cultures around the world have long recognized the therapeutic potential of sound. Instruments like Tibetan singing bowls, gongs, and Native American flutes have been used for centuries for meditation, spiritual connection, and healing.

When I prepared to train in the Seven Star Blessing Space Clearing™, I thought I knew all about space clearings and believed

I was a pro at smudging. What I didn't expect, though, was to fall in love with sound tools. I learned to use drums, bells, tingshas, gongs, and even singing bowls. When I discovered how to use these instruments to impact the energy of a space, I felt different. It wasn't like smoke wafting through the room; it was more powerful. I could literally hear the sound and instantly know if the space was clear or not. My favorite tool to use in my own home is my crystal singing bowl in the note of "F," which connects to the Heart Chakra. I adore the thought of infusing my home with more love.

If you're not ready to invest in any sound tools, you can experiment with what you have. Maybe you have an antique bell at home or your kids have a drum. You can also use the sound of your voice or even your own two hands to clap. I often clap in hotel rooms to clear out any negative energy from previous occupants. Keep clapping to break up the energy until it sounds clear and crisp. Don't forget, you can also access amazing playlists on Spotify and Apple Music. Crank up the volume and play!

Feeling excited to take on the senses with color, aroma and sound? These components may seem subtle, but they shape how we feel in our homes every single day.

CHAPTER 16

See It, Believe It, Live it

HAVE YOU EVER TRIED VISUALIZATION? Maybe you've experienced it in a yoga class, attempting to clear your mind, or perhaps you've developed your own meditation practice. But have you ever used visualization specifically for your home?

It's a fascinating way to connect with your space on a deeper level. Even just sitting quietly in your home and breathing can open your eyes to your space and how it's supporting you ... or not.

An important part of my Interior Alignment® consultation is the Synchro-Alignment™ guided visualization process. Created by Denise Linn, it's a unique way to experience your home. Through guided journeywork, you can learn about what your home has to tell you and what your soul truly needs in your most sacred space.

MEETING THE SPIRIT OF YOUR HOME

One of my favorite guided journeys is to assist the client in finding the essence or the spirit of their home. Some have elaborate, detailed experiences; others have simple experiences and connect with a color, shape or word.

My previous home had the essence of a man, "Lumber Jack John." He looked like Paul Bunyan, complete with plaid flannel shirt! My current home has the energy of a green pixie fairy. She's bright, cheerful, and so happy we're here.

While this visualization is a serious process, you need to know that whatever comes up is supposed to come up. One of my clients once connected with "The Count" from *Sesame Street* as the spirit of her home. We couldn't help but laugh but loved the joy and child-like feeling of this experience. Another client's home had the word "Love" in a beautiful script as its essence, while a third had a beautiful white silk fabric as their home spirit.

TRY THIS: A VISUALIZATION FOR CONNECTING WITH YOUR HOME

While I do the full guided journey with my clients, you can try this simplified version.

1. Find a quiet space where you won't be interrupted.

2. Sit in a chair in a comfortable position, legs uncrossed, and arms relaxed.

3. Allow your eyes to close and begin by connecting to your

breath. Take three deep and full belly breaths. This is where you inhale deeply and feel your belly expanding like a balloon and then let go.

4. After three rounds, take on some simple box breathing. Inhale for a count of four, hold for a count of four, release for a count of four, then hold for a count of four. Do a complete round of this three times.

5. Return your breathing back to its natural rhythm and let your mind wander. Imagine you're out in nature, experience it, absorb all the details of where you are. Maybe you're at a park, on a mountain or in a valley of flowers.

6. Imagine walking into your home. What are the first things that catch your eye? A piece of furniture, a family portrait, something else? Note what you see. From here continue to move about your space using your mind's eye.

7. Explore room by room. What do you love? What spaces make you uncomfortable? Take a general inventory.

8. Spend as long here as you'd like. When you feel ready, imagine returning to the magical spot in nature where you started. Take a few deep breaths. Then slowly add in some movements such as shrugging your shoulders or wiggling your fingers. When you're fully ready, you can open your eyes.

PROCESS YOUR EXPERIENCE

Take ten minutes to journal your experience. Write down everything you experienced—images, words, colors.

What did you see? What did you feel? Did your energy go higher or lower?

CHAPTER 17:

Tiny Tweaks, Big Shifts

WHEN I'M ASKED ABOUT THE EASIEST, fastest, most effective adjustments in a home—especially for busy, overwhelmed moms, I respond with a location you may pass by every day without a single thought: the front door.

THE FRONT DOOR: THE FIRST IMPRESSION

This front entry is so important. It's the first thing people see when they arrive at your home. What does it say? Would it convey the feeling of "We're overwhelmed with life and piles of shoes," or "This entry looks welcoming and inviting."

Your front door serves as a reflection of what you value most in life and what you hold dear. Does it feature symbols that represent your priorities and passions? Are visitors welcomed into a cozy space that smells inviting and feels like a warm embrace? Do the walls showcase family photos or artwork that highlights your interests and the pieces that bring you joy?

In Feng Shui, the front door is considered the "Mouth of Chi," the location where energy flows in. To be clear, this is the architectural front door, not the door most often used by you and your family.

If you're like most people, you typically use the garage or side entry when you come and go. This probably feels easier. In most homes, this is where the mud room, shoe storage, coat closet, and even bookbags can be dropped and some of that clutter can be hidden from guests. However, it's not the actual front door. So, while we want to do our best to keep these side and garage doors rather tidy and functional, the most important place to focus on is your actual front door.

You might be thinking, *Lisa, I can't use the front door when my car is in the garage!*

Get creative and come up with another reason to use the front door. You may plan to walk out to the mailbox every day or start your daily walk there. I helped my client, David, set up a system of taking his golden retriever on his walk through this front door by moving the leash and David's walking shoes to the front door coat closet.

I don't walk my dogs out my front door, but I do walk over each morning with my coffee in hand and step outside. I listen to the birds, look up at the sky to see what the weather looks like, and take three full and deep breaths, then I head back in.

NOTICE THE SHIFT

I find people instantly notice a major shift when making this adjustment of giving energy to your front door. This location is where energy flows into your home. It can also be an important area when you're looking to invite new opportunities into life. Looking for new friends, a life partner or that new job? This can be just the area to focus your attention on.

Take my client, Ana, who had a large walnut carved chest in front of her historic home's front door. The front door wasn't functioning well, and they eventually stopped using it and then placed the chest directly in front as if the door wasn't there. They sent guests to use the side door to enter where they would then have to climb over the shoes shoved in this small side entry.

When I shared with her how this could limit incoming opportunities, I saw a tear slide down her cheek. She explained that she'd been feeling stuck for a long time. Her teenage children were struggling in various ways, and her marriage wasn't much better. Her work had also hit the brakes in recent years. Nothing was going right.

We found the perfect place to move the chest— just across the room. Then Ana reached out to a handyman friend to help get the door repaired. We set up the plan that she was going to use the front door to get her mail. I suggested that while she does this, she slows down and takes a nice stroll down the drive and back to take in the beauty of her grand home, then carry that energy into her front door with her.

Ana soon felt lighter. Her husband started joining her on her "mail walks" occasionally, and her work started to pick up again. She said she felt an "overall shift and that life didn't feel so hard." She told me that she started to see the sunshine through the front door, and it reminded her why they fell in love with their historic home.

WHEN A DOOR PUSHES
OPPORTUNITIES AWAY

My husband and I have always enjoyed house hunting, whether we spent the day looking for a new rental property to add to our collection or simply touring an open house to explore a neighborhood or a new build. Heck, sometimes we even just wanted to see what a house looked like inside.

A while back, we were casually looking at some homes and we saw a listing for one that had been on the market for months. The price had dropped, and they were hosting an open house that day. We just had to go! We arrived at a beautiful ranch home with the scenic Florida intercoastal waterway just behind it. Pulling up, we were so curious about what we'd walk into. Why hadn't it sold? When we walked up to the entrance of the home, I knew immediately! The door opened outward instead of a traditional inward opening.

In Feng Shui, we always want a door to open inward and invite energy in. When the door opens out it diverts good luck. My Feng Shui sensors were on full speed as we entered.

The agent told us the seller was dealing with illness and obviously finances as they continued to drop the price with no offers. My Feng Shui "eyes" explored the home and layout, noticing several blaring issues: repairs needed at the center of the house (affecting health energy) and a straight-line path from the front door to the back door (often linked with financial instability).

The home eventually sold, but only after even more price reductions.

QUICK AND EASY FRONT DOOR CHECKLIST

- Sweep steps and entry regularly.

- Trim any overgrown greenery that impedes clear access to the front door.

- Refresh your front door mat if it's looking worn.

- Make sure the area is well lit. Does the knob and lock function well?

- Check door hinge functions to see if adjustments need to be made.

- Clean any glass panels or sidelights.

- Add decorative seasonal pots or flowers for color.

- Hang a beautiful welcome sign or decorative wreath on the door.

MY FRONT DOOR PET PEEVE

Few things frustrate me more than driving up and down the street repeatedly looking for a house number. I just want to give up and head home. In the past, I've even had to call clients to help me find their house.

After one of these particularly frustrating "tours" of a neighbor-hood, I found the home by process of elimination. House numbers were mounted on the house, but the shrubbery in front was so over-grown, there was absolutely no way to read them. If I can't find your house and the entrance, how will any prosperity be directed here? Surely, you'd want the local Girl Scout troop to easily locate your home, so they don't miss you on cookie delivery day, right?

Eventually, I started asking for several reference points such as the "brick two story" or "green shutters and black Volvo in the drive." Save your visitors the headache, and make sure your home number is easily visible.

It's easy to underestimate the power of small shifts in your home, but in the energetic language of the home, they speak volumes. Your front door is more than just an entry point; it's the threshold for opportunity, abundance, and fresh energy.

CHAPTER 18

The True North at Home

THE CENTER-MOST LOCATION of your dwelling holds the key to your health. In Feng Shui this is your home's health energy center. I like to call it "home base." To locate this, imagine being a bird in the sky with a view looking down over your home. What would be in the most interior area? This is your health energy center.

Finding it is simple. In many houses, it might be a hallway, stairwell, or even a closet. In other homes, it could be a living or dining room. Whatever it is, think of it like baseball: your goal is to make it to home base. If you've only got five minutes to improve your home's energy, this is where you want to go.

You may remember the story in an earlier chapter about David and his wife. They were dealing with their health and realized their clutter lived in their home's central area. With just a little effort, he was able to transform it into a space that supported balance and vitality.

If your home base happens to be in a main living area such as your dining or living room, keep it clean, clutter-free, and functional to support positive energy flow throughout. Bring in the earth element and colors of beige, tan, brown or yellow.

If your center is a closet, hallway, or stairway, you can still make a significant impact—just in different ways.

Ask yourself:

- Is it stored neatly?

- Does it represent abundance?

- Can it be more functional?

- Do I enjoy walking through or using this space?

In our Cleveland home, the health area was in a space you might not expect: a stairwell and pantry. At first glance, it didn't seem like there was much to adjust, but even stairwells can impact Chi, either slowing it down or making it rush too fast.

While we kept the space tidy, my husband had a habit of leaving small piles of items to go up or down, the classic *"grab a stack on your way"* pile. To create a more intentional flow, I placed a woven brown basket on the bottom step to neatly contain anything that needed to be moved and tried to empty it often.

The pantry, located on the back side of this area, required regular check-ins. Beyond clearing out expired food, I realized that quantity matters too. A nearly empty box of Cheerios lingering on the shelf doesn't reflect abundance. Instead, I started making a habit of using up the last handful and tossing the box, creating space for fresh, full replacements. Small shifts like these may seem simple, but they can enhance the energy of your home in powerful ways!

HOME BASE CHECKLIST

- Keep the space clutter free
- Remove expired items or worn-out items
- Refresh often to show abundance
- Keep the floors sparkling
- Replace any burnt-out lightbulbs
- Add mirrors to brighten dark hallways
- Make sure all doors open close smoothly

Remember, when the center of your home is clear, grounded, and energetically supported, it becomes a steady home base radiating harmony and vitality into every corner.

CHAPTER 19

The Sanctuary of Sleep

ACCORDING TO CFAH (The Center for Advancing Health), "Worldwide, 51% of the respondents in a global survey say that they're dissatisfied with the quality of their sleep.[6]" Sound familiar? Sleep challenges are the most common complaints I hear— tossing and turning, getting up to snack, feeling angry because of lack of sleep, and even resentment toward a partner who can get those solid eight hours.

In my experience, preparation for sleep seems to be the most beneficial followed by some important Feng Shui adjustments. Let's start with the preparation. Think of it this way: You can't go from driving your car 70 mph to hitting the brakes without a jarring

---

6   Nina Julia, "Sleep Statistics: Facts & Latest Data in America," January 11, 2024, https://cfah.org/sleep-statistics.

feeling and maybe smashing the eggs in the back seat. The same goes for your body. At the end of the day, or an especially busy day, take time to begin winding down long before it's your actual bedtime. A few hours before bed, begin to turn down the overhead lights and turn on the ambient glow of some small lamps. Sit with a cozy cup of herbal tea or a book to begin cueing to your body that it's nearing time for rest.

STOP THE SCROLL, I BEG YOU

Scrolling on your phone before bed might seem harmless, but it's working against you. The blue light tricks your body into thinking it's still daytime, throwing off your natural sleep cycle. And let's be honest, we've all been there. One minute, you're just checking messages, and the next, you're adding another pair of jeans to your cart or getting lost in a rabbit hole of videos. Swapping screen time for a relaxing bedtime routine can make all the difference in how well you sleep.

MY FAVORITE SLEEP PREP HELPERS

- One of my favorite "tools" is a Himalayan salt lamp. It provides effective health benefits if you battle with allergies because they help clean the air. They also provide a beautiful, soft glow. On most nights, around 8:00 PM I start dimming the overhead lights and turn on small lamps and a few of these salt lamps located around my home. There's no denying their warm and soothing glow. They release negative ions that bring balance to the high number of positive ions (because of all the electrical items) throughout our homes. Try one. I know you'll like it.

- My next personal sleep prep advice is to invest in high quality bedding. Some clients tell me they don't feel the need to invest in quality bedding because "no one sees it," and "they're just sleeping while in there." You *deserve* quality bedding. This can serve as a reflection of how you view yourself. *You are worthy* of sleeping blissfully on luxury sheets with pillows that make you melt. Must you have a custom duvet made or buy an outrageous thread count of sheets? No. But buy the best quality that you can afford and take some time to intentionally create a lovely experience. Upgrade your sheets if they're beginning to look worn and pilling, and buy some fresh pillows. Layer on some blankets for varying temperatures and always opt for texture when selecting blankets.

- My third personal fave is essential oils for aromatherapy. Essential oils come directly from plants and are usually extracted through steam distillation. Aromatherapy works by inhaling these natural scents, helping to shift energy and support your well-being. Since smell has a direct impact on sleep, bringing specific essential oils into your bedtime routine can be a simple yet powerful way to improve rest and relaxation.

- My favorite essential oil is lavender, but there are many others that induce relaxation, such as Chamomile, Bergamot,

Cedarwood, Frankincense, and Clary Sage. I recommend my clients snag an oil or two as well as a diffuser for their bedroom. Diffusers can be purchased rather inexpensively. The oils, on the other hand, can be pricier depending on the exact oil. Steer clear of those oils on the end cap of the discount store whose price seems too good to be true. Instead, look for a reputable brand that sells high quality oils that state they are made of 100% essential oil and that no fillers or fragrances were added. I use several brands but particularly love the DoTerra line. Remember to do your research online and read reviews.

BEDROOM FENG SHUI BASICS

Now for the nuts and bolts of bedroom Feng Shui. First, place your bed in the command position where the bed is ideally placed along a solid wall with a clear view of the entry door off to one side, not directly opposite the door. Having your feet directly in line with the door places you in the "corpse position" which just sounds as awful as it is energetically. Always avoid having any view into the bathroom too, especially a view of the toilet. Close the bathroom door or rearrange the bed if needed.

Sleeping under a sloped ceiling or under a beam can disrupt your energy. Over the years, whenever I've had a client reach out who suffers from migraines they're often sleeping under a beam or sloped roof. Position your bed so these aren't overhead.

Looking to decorate? Incorporate soothing and restful artwork and avoid collections of family photographs. Family portraits are often displayed in the master bedroom, but these are more appropriate for the public areas of the home. Reserve the master bedroom for just the adults.

TVS AND MIRRORS: SLEEP DISRUPTERS

I see them all the time in bedrooms. I get it, when you're trying to relax, sometimes watching TV does the trick. Here is the issue, though. Both TVs and mirrors have shiny, reflective surfaces that can disrupt sleep. They also carry a lot of energy. For example, think of the last TV show you watched? Was it calming, peaceful, and restful, or was it a movie with a dramatic high speed car chase? This type of energy won't support you in getting your needed rest.

I encourage you to experiment with removing your TV from the bedroom. Give it six weeks, then check in to see how your sleep may have improved. If you absolutely must have a television in the bedroom, I recommend placing it in a cabinet with doors that close to hide it when you're finished using it. If you already have it mounted on the wall, opt for throwing a scarf or draping a piece of pretty fabric over the TV for sleep.

As for mirrors? Most people want a quick view before heading out in the morning.

But think about this. They hold onto energy from past owners (just like antiques), and they hold onto energy from you and your experience using it. Remember the last time you tried on that dress from ten years ago that you'd hoped you'd fit into by now but don't? Those negative feelings or unkind self-talk are embedded in that mirror. I recommend replacing that mirror above your dresser with a beautiful piece of art. Swap the full-length mirror with something else beautiful and decorative that says, "restful retreat."

So where do you place a mirror? I recommend you relocate the mirror to the closet.

WHAT'S UNDER YOUR BED?

While it might seem like the perfect spot to stash luggage, old shoes, or out-of-season clothes, it's not the ideal place for storage. Think about it. You're spending six to eight hours every night, 365 days a year sleeping right on top of that energy. That's a lot of time to be absorbing whatever is beneath you.

And here's the real question: What are you storing? A pair of jeans you hope to fit into someday? Old photos from a past relationship? The energy of these items lingers and can impact you whether you realize it or not. Clearing out the space under your bed creates room for better sleep, clearer energy, and fresh possibilities.

My client Laura contacted me because she was having trouble sleeping. We discussed a few details about her bedroom, and then I finally asked her, "Can I peek underneath your bed?" She chuckled and said, "Oh sure, there's just storage underneath." She slowly pulled out several piles of books that she'd planned to read "when life slowed down." She then pulled out boxes of printed photos she was planning on putting into an album. She was "hoping to get to this project soon." You see, while she was supposed to be resting, she was sleeping on top of a "to-do" list. No wonder she was having a hard time. I advised her to remove all the storage and keep nothing under her bed.

THE BEDROOM AS A STRESS DUMP: RENEE'S STORY

Renee has always been a busy woman who loved her fast-paced work and life. She also loved returning to her cozy ranch-style home at the end of the day.

Over the past year though, she began to struggle with sleep. She once loved her bedroom, but now it felt overwhelming. No matter how many meditation apps she downloaded or herbal teas she sipped, Renee tossed and turned every night. Each morning, she was exhausted and irritable.

After visiting her home and viewing her bedroom, I saw a cluttered bedside table and a stack of books piled ten high. In the corner was a basket of laundry to be folded, while another basket of laundry had "exploded" onto a nearby chair. She also had a small table that held her computer and a stack of her client files.

Her bedroom had become a storage space for her stress where she dumped her unfinished work projects and piles of laundry. No wonder it didn't feel restful. However, she didn't see it until I explained it. The piles of "to do" were keeping her up at night.

The client files, unfolded laundry, and piles of books were subconsciously telling her that it wasn't safe to go to sleep, that she had too much to do before sleep. No wonder she was frustrated. I helped her devise a plan to move these projects and tasks to another area of the home. I advised her to leave the single book that she's currently reading on the bedside table, and that's it. We also addressed the random clutter in the room.

Our goal was to tidy up intentionally. We brought in a fresh set of sheets in a soft beige color to really symbolize resetting to a grounding energy and added a softer bedside table lamp and even a Himalayan Salt lamp in the corner. We infused this room with calm and serenity. Renee is no longer battling sleep but falling softly into a peaceful slumber.

EXERCISE EQUIPMENT SENDS ME OVER THE EDGE

I get it. Sometimes you're tight on space if you're in an apartment or smaller home. However, I've learned that sleep is a challenge for so many people. If you're having problems with sleep, you know it impacts nearly every aspect of your life.

I can't begin to count how many times I've walked into a client's bedroom who has difficulty with sleep, and I'm instantly greeted by workout equipment. Here's what I want you to understand. Sleep is a quiet, peaceful event. It's very yin in energy, and working out is the exact opposite. It's more of a "working" or "doing" energy.

Picture this: You're spinning on the bike incredibly fast, your legs are on fire, and sweat is sliding down your neck. You ask yourself; *Do I stop for a water break?* You tell yourself, *No, keep going.* You might be watching other spinners or a coach on a screen encouraging you to "push harder" or "dig deeper."

I'm all about this amped up excited energy, and it keeps me going on a long workout, but this type of energy is not conducive to rest and relaxation. Even after the workout is over, having the treadmill simply sitting in your room hours after you completed your workout still affects the energy of the space and your body. It shifts your restful bedroom retreat into a multipurpose room. Let's take it back to that blissful sleep oasis, shall we? Transfer those high energy, active workouts to a more active room in your home.

BEDROOM CHECKLIST FOR BETTER SLEEP

- Place your headboard against a solid wall.

- Have a clear view of the entry door.

- Make sure you don't have items stored under your bed.

- Keep "active" items such as treadmills and computers out of the bedroom.

- Invest in quality bedding you love.

- Swap out your mirror for restful, relaxing art.

- Add blackout or room darkening blinds if needed.

- Add soft lamps or a Himalayan salt lamp to your bedroom for lighting options.

Remember, getting prepared and setting your space up for nourishing sleep is key. Create that bedroom you've always dreamed of!

CHAPTER 20

The Soul of the Home

KITCHENS CAN BE ONE OF THOSE SPACES that people love or just see as a headache. If you're a foodie and you love to cook, you may be that person who can't wait to get home and pull out the ingredients and get to work. Or you may be like me who's just not interested in cooking elaborate meals. Maybe you just see the kitchen as a place where you feel stress about what to make or how you'll handle picky eaters.

In any case, I want you to consider this: **Your kitchen is where you nourish your body and the bodies of those you love.** Go ahead. Read it again and let that sink in.

FENG SHUI IN THE KITCHEN: BALANCING THE ELEMENTS

In Feng Shui, kitchens are known for representing nourishment while also influencing relationships, wealth and abundance, and so much more. Here's an example: The stove (which represents the fire element) and the sink (introduces the water element) symbolize powerful yet opposing energies. You see, fire embodies warmth, passion, and transformation, while water symbolizes fluidity, emotion, and clarity. When these two elements are positioned directly next to each other, it can create energetic tension. This may lead to feelings of conflict, stress, or instability within the home.

To harmonize this, introduce the wood element for balance. The wood element serves as a natural bridge between fire and water, offering a sense of growth and stability. An easy solution is to place a wooden cutting board, a bamboo tray, or even a small plant between the stove and sink. The wood element helps to absorb excess energy and promotes a peaceful, supportive atmosphere in your kitchen.

If space allows, you can also incorporate wood through decorative items, such as a wooden bowl filled with fresh fruit or a small wooden shelf for herbs and spices. These simple additions not only create balance but are also attractive.

YOUR STOVE: A SYMBOL OF ABUNDANCE

In Feng Shui, the stove serves as a powerful symbol of wealth and prosperity. It's not just an appliance for cooking meals; it can be a magnet for abundance. To harness its full potential, make sure all burners are in perfect working order. A broken or unused burner can symbolize missed opportunities and stagnant energy. Fix or replace any that aren't functioning. Rotate the use of your burners regularly. Each burner represents a different avenue for wealth and opportunity, so when you switch things up, you're activating all potential pathways for prosperity. This is a simple yet powerful way to keep abundant energy flowing into your life.

Don't forget to keep the stovetop clean and clutter-free. A sparkling stove not only promotes clarity but also invites fresh energy into your home. Make it a mindful practice to wipe it down after each use, setting an intention for wealth, health, and happiness.

INFUSING FOOD WITH POSITIVE ENERGY

When you can realize the connection you have to everything you put in your body, from the vegetables you lovingly chop to the stew on the range that you give a gentle stir to, it takes on something different.

For your next meal, consider the energy you're fusing into it. Are you simply standing at the kitchen island shoveling in food to get to your next activity, or are you slowing down to pull out a proper napkin and sitting down to actually taste your food? You might not need to do this every day, but think about ways you might enhance nourishment of your body.

MY RITUALS FOR NOURISHMENT

One of my favorite ways to slow down is to make my morning coffee and sit in my favorite chair. With each sip I take, I feel the warm liquid going down and take in the aroma. I also use this time to slow down, look at the birds out the window for just a couple minutes. I also try to plan a proper dinner during the week. My husband travels on business, so there are many nights when I just need to make dinner for myself. Not going to lie, I've had a few PB&J nights and often a quickly thrown together salad or scrambled eggs. But at least once a week I sit down to the table. I set the table and pull out a cloth napkin. I might pull out a wine glass just to add my water to it and use my nice china. For the meal, I'll typically make one of my favorite salmon or veggie dishes. While chopping or stirring I'll recite a mantra to the food—"Peace, Love, and Nourishment"— or even send Reiki energy over my plate just before eating. It feels so nourishing to feed both my body and spirit.

TIPS TO INFUSE YOUR FOOD WITH GOOD ENERGY

- Pull out the "nice" dishes on a regular day.

- Use cloth napkins (better for the environment, and amps up the experience).

- Prepare your food with high quality, organic ingredients and opt for healthier options.

- Stir or chop while reciting your favorite mantra, poem or prayer.

- Light a candle on your table.

- Use a fancy glass for your beverage.

- Turn on some relaxing music to play in the background.

- Pause to taste your food. What are the flavors and textures, and how are they mixed?

As we leave the warmth of the kitchen, we carry forward the understanding that design is not only about function but about energy. When this space is aligned, it uplifts the entire home.

CHAPTER 21:
Small Spaces, Big Magic

SMALL SPACES CAN BE SOME OF THE MOST fascinating and rewarding environments to design. Whether you live in a compact condo, a miniscule New York City apartment, tiny home, or even an RV, bringing harmony to tight quarters often has a surprising impact.

I recently met Alex, who lives full-time traveling in her RV. She describes her experience like this: "I love my RV. It's roughly 200 sq. ft of MINE. One thing I don't love is not feeling grounded. Living on wheels, no matter how much you stabilize it, feels unsteady."

She was spot on. Even when the RV is parked, she's still technically on wheels and not grounded. I always remind my nomadic clients of the importance of being extra intentional about grounding. Simple practices—walking barefoot outside, spending more time in nature, or surrounding yourself with natural elements— can help immensely. Inside the RV, bringing in rocks, crystals, or even a beautiful clay pottery piece as a centerpiece can anchor the energy and create a stronger sense of stability no matter where you're headed.

So maybe your space is snug, but not RV snug. Even a small apartment can be made to feel so much more airy and open with a few tweaks. Add some Feng Shui, and you can create one cozy little nest.

LOVE STORY IN A LIVING ROOM

One of the sweetest moments was when I worked with my close friend, Lindsey, in her condo. A marriage proposal from her longtime boyfriend Andrew was on the top of her wish list. They'd discussed at length, but it just wasn't happening.

By intentionally rearranging a few pieces of furniture in her living room and adding a beautiful plant along with some cues representing love into her condo, her wish came true. In fact, Andrew proposed in the living room, the same room that we'd worked on!

ENTRY POINTS MATTER

Optimizing your home's entry is vital in a small space. Just a few items can block the flow and make the space feel chaotic. Keeping your entry tidy and organized is crucial. Even a wall shelf to collect keys and mail or a small cabinet to store bags and purses keep things tidy. Opt for narrow pieces and even better, curved pieces for a more welcoming feeling.

Make sure, however, that as you decorate and add storage that nothing impedes the door from opening fully. After all, even in an apartment, the front door to your unit is your "mouth of chi." Make sure the door opens fully and easily to allow in new opportunities. Want to make your entry feel even bigger? A mirror can help. Just make sure it doesn't reflect the front door directly, or it might send the energy right back out! Place it where it reflects something you really love too.

FURNISHING FOR FLOW

Today's furniture options are wonderfully adaptable for small spaces, especially choices with hidden storage available. Think functional and flexible—pieces that can easily be folded or stacked, such as an extra folding end table that can slide behind the sofa when not in use and a sleeper sofa for guests. Looking for larger pieces such as upholstered sofas or chairs? Choose pieces with more rounded rather than squared and boxy shapes. This improves the energy flow and helps avoid bumps when trying to navigate a room when serving a tray of drinks. I also recommend upholstered pieces with exposed feet versus skirting that goes to the floor to create a more spacious and open feeling.

Storage ottomans are one of my favorite pieces to add to a room. They're practical, stylish, and multifunctional. I particularly like the small cube ottomans where you lift the lid and find all kinds of space inside for blankets, remotes, books, or whatever you want to store. They're also easy to move for extra seating.

SMART STORAGE WITH STYLE

In general, storage can be a real puzzle, right? Years ago, while launching my first interior design business, I took a part time gig with Closet

Factory. I needed to make some money and was genuinely excited to learn all the smart storage tricks. Wow, what an adventure!

We weren't just organizing closets; we were designing luxurious dressing rooms, craft areas, laundry rooms, and the most drool-worthy pantries. Picture this: storage bins, drawers, dividers, shelves, perfectly sized baskets, and even special inserts just for your bag of potatoes. Yes, seriously, potato baskets! During my time there, I learned so much about the art of storage and how to create systems that make life easier—and prettier.

If you've never considered custom closets, consider this your official permission slip.

These companies literally have it down to a science of how many ladies' sweaters can be stored on their shelves and exactly how to stack them. They count every pair of pants and dresses you own and measure the height of your favorite high heels! It's brilliant.

I also learned the importance of going vertical. Often, there's unused space at the top of the closet. You may want to put this book down, go to a closet and look up. What do you see? Wasted space? There may be a shelf there. Can you add another on top? You might be thinking, *How will I get the items when I need them?* No worries. This storage is for those rarely used items—the off-season winter boots or holiday decorations. And you can always buy a lightweight step stool.

I also love to bring in vertical storage into a main area of the home such as a living room or bedroom with narrow, floating shelves. Stacking three or five artistically can look attractive but also provide a landing space for those candles, picture frames, or knick knacks. And consider trying vintage ladders! You can usually find one at your local antique store. They're not only charming but also super practical. Need a spot for extra bedding for your sofa bed? Simply drape neatly folded blankets over the ladder rungs. You can also add hooks to hang baskets from the rungs, perfect for storing books, coasters, remotes, or whatever your heart desires.

PLANTS AND LIGHTS: SOFTENING THE SPACE

Plants can be invaluable in making you feel comfortable and at home. Whether you're in an RV or in a condo, some small plants are just the thing to bring life into your environment. Plants connect to the wood element of Feng Shui and inspire an energy of healing, renewal, and growth. Get creative with a climbing vine if you have tall ceilings or stick to smaller plants. Be careful, though. Don't go overboard on size and quantity, or your space will feel even smaller. Plus, too many plants can bring too much wood energy. Remember, for good Feng Shui, opt for plants with soft, rounded leaves and always avoid cactus.

THINK NEUTRAL

When it comes to color in small spaces, light neutrals are your best friend. Color can easily make a space feel smaller or larger. You may be thinking, *Hmm … What about an accent wall to bring in a color without being overwhelming?* I typically say yes in a larger space but think twice in snug spaces. Painting a single wall can easily change the shape of the room to feel more skinny or narrow. What once felt as a somewhat spacious area can instantly feel closed in. Focus on those basic neutral colors and bring in some accents. Infuse some interest to the walls with neutral textured wallpaper for a cozy feeling.

WINDOW TREATMENTS THAT WORK

Window treatments can be complicated (Don't even get me started on the RV pre-installed blinds. Ick). In a small space, though, you may not have many windows, the window's casing may be awkward and not allow for many options in type, styling or hardware, or the window placement on the wall may simply be bizarre.

LISA'S FAVORITE NEUTRAL COLORS

Sherwin Williams—Alabaster

Sherwin Williams—Egret White

Sherwin Williams—Agreeable Gray

Benjamin Moore—Chantilly Lace

Farrow & Ball—Shaded White

My go-to solution? Soft, breezy sheer or casual linen panels. Hang the rod as close to the ceiling, and make sure you have enough fabric so it nearly touches the floor. If you're having them custom made, I always recommend 1/2" off the floor. The soft feeling of these sheer or neutral panels softens the harsh lines of the window casing so the room feels more like an oasis. Installing them high also elongates the wall and may make the ceiling appear taller. If you need to add some sort of window treatment for privacy or light filtering, add a 2" wood blind. They install rather easily, look clean and neat, and can provide just the amount of privacy and light filtering. And they'll complement your decorative panels.

DECLUTTERING: THE REAL
GAME-CHANGER

In a small space, just a few pieces of clutter can scream. Do you remember that scene in the movie *27 Dresses* where Katherine Heigel's bridesmaid dress closet was bursting so much she could barely close it? In a 5000 sq. ft home, 27 dresses (albeit puffy, layered, and tiered) may fit more easily in the closet space, but a tiny home? No way!

Here's my no-fail rule to minimize clutter: One in, one out. So, you're buying a new pair of pink casual sneakers? The green ones have to go. You bought a new set of serving bowls? Donate the old ones.

If you don't know where to begin, start with your clothing. Do you really need five pairs of black pants, or will two suffice? If you don't often have guests stay overnight, is there a need for two extra comforters, or will one work?

Edit where you can. Sentimental clutter can be especially tricky. Consider storing sentimental family items off site—maybe another family member's home or in safe storage. Are the things you're storing really valuable, or do you just kind of like them? If they're not truly warming your heart, consider donating or repurposing them. My husband, for example, had a whole collection of NBA freebie T-shirts he wasn't willing to part with. Were they valuable? Only to him because of his memories. Guess what? I had my friend make them into a custom t-shirt quilt. I loved decluttering the closet, and he loved his gift.

As we bring spaciousness, intention, and flow into our homes, no matter the square footage, we need to remember that we aren't the only ones living there. Our homes are shared sanctuaries, and for many of us, that includes our beloved pets. These furry, feathered, or four-legged companions feel energy just as deeply as we do, and they rely on the environments we create to feel safe, calm, and at home. In the next chapter, we'll explore how to honor their presence through Feng Shui and intuitive design choices that nurture both their well-being and yours.

CHAPTER 22:
Whiskers, Paws, and Good Chi

PETS ARE OFTEN THE HEART OF A HOME. I've always had a soft spot for animals—especially dogs. My two English Mastiffs, Cub and Violet, make frequent appearances on my social media feeds. Whether you're a dog person, cat lover, or have a lizard, guinea pig, or fish, pets bring joy, warmth, and an unmistakable sense of love to a space.

There's no denying the feeling when you enter your home after a long day and your dog's tail is wagging uncontrollably. If you're not a pet person because you travel, have inconsistent schedules, or just don't have the bandwidth for another family member, no worries. Maybe you know someone with pets, or maybe someday you'll have one.

Here are some ideas to keep both you and your furry (or scaly!) friend happy at home.

DESIGN TIPS FOR
PET-FRIENDLY LIVING

Flooring: Practical and Durable

Keep it simple. Pet nails and wood floors don't mix. You're probably not going to be happy when your sweet chocolate lab scratches up the new hardwood floor you installed. Tile and the popular and waterproof LVT (luxury vinyl tile) are wise options. This is one of my go-tos for families with young kiddos and pets. The planks wear beautifully, and if one gets damaged, the plank can easily be removed and replaced.

If you do opt for hardwood, be aware there will be scratches. Dogs love to play; it's in their nature to run and jump around.

Color: Go Natural

While we consider our pets precious family members, they are animals and ultimately want to connect to nature. We may want to surround them with pink fluff, but a simple beige or tan bed will make them just as happy.

Instead of splurging on a purple sequined collar, think about what would make them happy if they were out in the wild. What colors and materials would they like? Most often natural colors: beige, tan, brown, and green.

COMMAND POSITION: PETS LIKE POWER SPOTS TOO

Just as it benefits us humans to be in the command position, your pets feel the effects too. Try to place their bed against a solid wall with a view of the room's entry. They'll feel more comfortable, confident and relaxed.

Tuning into Pet Energy

Pets are incredibly sensitive to energy. Is there a room your pet won't go in? Is there a place where they love to spend time? Watch your pets, and you'll learn a great deal about the energy of your home. I especially love having clients watch their pets just before and after a space clearing!

Animals are so special that we want to go above and beyond to care for them and please them. I recently heard how many homeless people will feed their dog before they feed themselves. I'm not surprised. I once had clients design in white to match their dog's fur color. The carpet was white; their sofa was white, everything!

So often, we want to do everything to make our pets comfortable—especially when they're aging or sick. Believe me, I can relate to that. But we have to be careful. We need to live healthy lives, too.

LINDA'S STORY

Linda booked an appointment with me, then canceled and rescheduled twice. The third time I knew something was going on. Sure, sometimes people need to cancel and reschedule, but this felt different.

When I arrived at her beautiful brick home nestled in the woods, Linda greeted me with a smile. She invited me in and apologized for the previous cancellations. We walked into her home, and I was utterly confused. There was no construction happening anywhere, yet there was plastic sheeting covering every horizontal surface: plastic covered the flooring and rugs, the sofa and chairs, even the carpeted stairwell. My initial thought was that Linda didn't appear physically stable, and I was fearful she was going to trip on the plastic.

When we sat down, she immediately mentioned the plastic and apologized for it. I asked her to tell me about it. She explained she was a cat lover and recently lost one of her cats. Now she's contending with her one remaining cat. He was old, nearing the end of his life, and vomiting often. Her solution was covering all the surfaces in plastic.

Linda couldn't maneuver around to clean as quickly as she'd like. Sometimes, she'd even miss a spot and not know it was there until the next day.

She shared even more as we sat casually at her kitchen dining table. Her husband had passed years before, and recently she lost her only son. Add to that her previous loss of her cat and now her last family member, this aging cat, was ill. Linda was devastated and hung tightly onto this last family member. Her home had stopped being a home; it had become a cat hospice.

I asked where the cat liked to spend most of its time. "The sunroom," she said. "She loves watching the birds." And Linda's favorite place? The sunroom, where she loved reading her Bible. What a perfect place to create a sanctuary for the two.

I talked Linda into creating a special retreat in her sunroom for the two of them. We rearranged the furniture, brought in all the cat toys and the litter box, and then opened the blinds. Here, they could snuggle, watch the birds, and she could read her bible. Because the cat would spend most of her time in the sunroom, Linda would know where she was, and the messes would be contained.

Best of all, no more plastic! Linda could enjoy her home, go back to hosting guests, and really living in the spaces. I encouraged her to find some areas of the home that she wanted to connect with such as trying some new recipes in the kitchen or sewing in the living room.

My goal with Linda was to create an energy of connection and special moments with this cat, not to enhance the energy of loss and illness in her home. We could celebrate the here and now and explore what lights her up beside her cat.

Designing with pets in mind isn't just about scratch-proof floors and washable fabrics. It's about honoring their place in our hearts and creating spaces that deepen our bond.

CHAPTER 23:

Guarding the Spirit of Your Space

THE POWER OF PEOPLE IN YOUR SPACE

You might already understand how a guest's energy can impact the overall harmony of your home. Perhaps you have that one family member whose presence seems to bring everyone down, such as an uncle who's always negative and eager to spread his misery.

While being mindful of the friends and family we welcome into our sacred space is crucial, have you ever considered the energy of those who aren't part of your inner circle?

Years ago, while doing design work in Cleveland, I partnered with my favorite general contractor, Ryan—a delightful second-generation business owner. He'd show up in his bright red truck, rather wild beard and tattoos, and I'd have to jokingly remind him not to swear too much during his first meeting with my clients. In the end, my clients always fell in love with him, repeatedly, remarking "Ryan is amazing" and "Ryan is simply the best."

His entire crew was wonderful too. He set the stage for success with his attitude and wouldn't tolerate anyone not performing their best. Our values were similar, so we were a perfect match. I'd arrive onsite with a car full of light fixtures, and his guys would be there to carry things in before I could get the car in park. They were kind to me, but again, most important to my client.

One client lost her husband to cancer just after we completed a project. You'd never have known what this cheerful man was dealing with. I cherish the thought that while he was fighting cancer, we were putting beautiful finishes and materials and good vibes into his home for his wife to enjoy.

Another favorite memory was working with Mr. and Mrs. Vara. He was a retired music teacher; she was a retired home economics teacher (or as it's currently known, family and consumer science). She always had freshly baked goods for the crew, and they hosted a barbecue for the team. I believe when you put positive energy into your work, it's always returned.

BUT ALL EXPERIENCES AREN'T POSITIVE

A few projects I'm happy to forget. I once worked with a client who hired me to design their space and collaborate with a remodeler they'd already brought onboard even though I'd recommended Ryan.

The husband-and-wife clients of this mid-century modern home were fantastic. Unfortunately, the contractor referred to me as "girl" for the entire summer. I observed his shortcuts and lack of proper permitting. Clearly, he wasn't invested in delivering quality work or treating these kind homeowners with the respect they deserved. That experience taught me an important lesson: to be selective about who I collaborate with, even if it's someone the client initially prefers.

Once I had to do something I never imagined: repossess furniture and accessories from a client's office. She was a dentist who refused to pay me, a dentist who was undoubtedly being handsomely compensated for her dental work. Unbelievable. Thankfully though, my incredible friend, Ali, stepped in to help. She helped me move the furniture out and kept me calm and positive while the dentist's office manager glared at us.

A month later, I saw them post photos online of the "new look" of the office that directly mimicked what I had done—similar furniture, layout, and even artwork. This experience was a tough but another valuable lesson about trusting my gut when deciding which clients to take on. In the past, I wanted to make everyone happy and say yes to every opportunity, but I've learned that not every opportunity is worth pursuing. It's not worth my energy trying to work with someone who operates with ill intentions.

LESSONS LEARNED

1. **Trust Your Gut.** Whatever you feel is right. You're not overthinking.

2. **Lead with Positive Energy.** Showing genuine care, kindness, and support of emotions, physical and financial concerns is vital.

3. **Work with Positive Professionals.** Every screw they tighten, every fixture they install, and every plank of wood they lay is infused with positive energy.

HIRING WITH INTENTION

Here's some advice when hiring everyone from electricians to plumbers, installers to refinishers.

1. Do Your Research

We all appreciate referrals, but do your homework. Did your friend actually use that company, or did they just hear their name somewhere? Ask questions and get several referrals.

- See if the firm has a website, photos of projects, information on the owners and/or staff, and background on the company. (I personally love multi-generational family business stories.)

- Call and chat with them. If they want your business, they'll give you time to discuss your project or at least a quick, casual discussion. Keep in mind it also gives them an opportunity to ensure that you are a good fit for them. It's a win-win. Don't be afraid to ask lots of questions. More than likely, they'll love to share their passion with you too.

I fully understand that you've decided to take on a large project and you're incredibly excited to get it started. But slow down. I've heard several stories from people not doing their research. This includes horrible paint jobs with the wrong colors to the floor being laid in the wrong direction, and even a home robbery.

2. Set Clear Expectations

A remodel is *not* easy. Removing tile can be incredibly dirty, sanding floors can be dusty, heck—even just having the brown protective paper down on the walkways can be annoying. Did I mention all the noise? You certainly can't plan to work from home and be productive while crews are there pounding on the walls. So, before the first tradesperson even arrives on-site, set realistic expectations.

- Your home will get dirty. Remember, it can be cleaned.

- Noise will sometimes be an issue. Don't think you're going to do any relaxing yoga or take part on a conference call while the crew is working.

- Your life will feel a bit messy.

- Add additional time onto your project completion date no matter what you are told. Things happen: Faucets may arrive in the wrong finish; the light fixture may arrive broken in shipping. Expect some hiccups. They're often beyond anyone's control, or at least anyone's on your jobsite team. Rely on those making the decisions for support such as your designer about the best resolutions.

Here's a unique story. One client endured a full kitchen and dining room remodel by choosing sardines as their gourmet sustenance. Yes, I said sardines. While we'd scheduled the update for their culinary haven during the summer so they could grill outside, they knew what they were in for and stocked up on easy and quick foods such as sardines. They also planned to visit some recently opened restaurants they wanted to check out. Personally, I'd never be on board with sardines, but sign me up for the new restaurants.

So, set your expectations appropriately. Keeping your head in the game will help you stay in the right headspace and retain your home's energy and harmony.

3. Prepare Your Home (and Yourself)

This process begins the moment we decide to move forward on a project.

Declutter

Pack away decorative and valuable items to protect them and avoid accidents. Take your time to safely pack them away yourself so you know they're safe and secure, even if someone on the crew offers to help.

Pack away any valuables: money, jewelry, and medications. Even with the best intentions on everyone's part, sometimes someone may have a bad day and not make a good decision.

- Most often, the remodelers will move any furniture, but if you have specific needs, handle this on your own. I have a nearly 300 LB Himalayan Salt Lamp that can be a bit top heavy when moving. We always move this ourselves to avoid anyone getting hurt.

- Update your routines. This may mean coming and going through a different entry or adding ten minutes to talk to the trades onsite before heading out the door to work.

  - **Kitchen remodel?** Stock up on quick and easy food.

  - **Master bathroom update?** Move your toiletries to another bathroom for the time being.

  - **Working from home?** Rent an office space for the time being, check out a local co-working venue or opt for a coffee shop or the public library.

4. Charging Your Space

During building, remodeling and redecorating, there are many opportunities to infuse your home with ceremony, love, and care. Just like charging your crystals, it's giving the energy of your home a task or a project.

Here are some suggestions:

Write a letter to your home and place it in the foundation.
When building a new home and you're visiting the jobsite early on, ask yourself, "What do I really want for this new space?"

I had a client who was building a large two-story home, and they and their three children wrote on notecards what they wanted for their family in their home. They placed their cards among the framing of the house.

Use Crystals

Find stones that represent your intentions and then bury those beautiful pieces of earth around the home or foundation. My favorite stone for this is rose quartz, the stone of love and compassion. You can bury rose quartz with the intention of love for your family as well as gifting the stone to your home. I also love black tourmaline for protection, hematite for grounding, and citrine for positivity. Many other stones may work for you, depending on your home's layout, but these three are a strong starting point.

Write on the Walls If You're Doing a Refresh

Before painting, you can take a pen and (depending on the color you're painting the wall) write on the wall. Infuse it with symbolism such as hearts or peace signs; write a prayer, poem, or mantra on the wall. I love to write this quote by author and artist Mary Anne Radmacher-Hershey: "May your walls know joy, may every room hold laughter, and every window open to great possibility."

These images and words will then be painted over, but the beautiful words and symbolism you applied will be infused into the wall permanently.

5. Cleanse Your Home After Construction

As I advised earlier, find a team or crew of good, kind humans. However, we are just that—humans. Someone may have a bad day.

Accidents may happen. Someone may get injured in your home. The installer who just arrived may have just had an argument with his wife on his drive to your house. Sure, he doesn't intend to bring that energy into your home, but even by lunchtime, he continues to stew. That argumentative energy and stressed energy is now in your space.

This is why I recommend you cleanse the energy of your entire home after any trades are finished, and you've moved furniture, accessories, and your great aunt's figurine collection to its home.

Tips to Clear Lingering Energy

- **Smudge** with a burnable item such as white sage, sweetgrass or palo santo.

- **Use sound tools** such as tingshas, bells or singing bowls throughout to vibrate the energy and cleanse.

- **Use rocks and crystals** to refresh the energy of the space. My favorite is amethyst because it purifies energy, is a natural cleanser, and serves as a shield against negativity.

Your home is your sanctuary. Protect it by being intentional about who enters, how it's treated, and what kind of energy lives there. Every detail matters, from the people you hire, to the way you prepare, cleanse, and bless your space.

CHAPTER 24

Breathing Life into Your Home

AS YOU READ IN CHAPTER 1 of this book, your home isn't just a box or a physical structure; it holds energy. In addition to the items you bring in, this energy is shaped by the experiences, events, and interactions that take place inside.

You may take on a remodel project to align your home with your goals, maybe repaint your master bedroom to improve your sleep, for example. Or maybe you're planning to build your dream home and can take that on with all the tips and advice you've read in this book to bring your dreams to fruition.

When I think about the process of shaping a home, I'm reminded of a French saying I adore: *"Petit à petit, l'oiseau fait son nid."*

"Little by little, the bird makes its nest."

This quote deeply resonates with me, especially when I think about creating a home that truly supports and reflects who you are. It reminds us that creating beauty, a sense of comfort, and alignment in our home, doesn't have to be rushed or perfect. What matters is doing it with intention. Over time, these little adjustments add up to create the sanctuary you've been longing for.

INTRODUCING NESTORATIONS

Consider this: You have the power to infuse your home with the essence you crave through simple, sweet, loving actions. I call these "Nestorations." You may have heard of people talking about "glimmers," those small moments that spark joy or peace in your day. Nestorations work the same way, inviting you to delightfully sprinkle vibes into your sweet nest or home.

A Nestoration isn't just about cleaning, tidying up, or making Feng Shui adjustments, it's about mindfully caring for your home in ways that feel nurturing. It's the difference between rushing through chores and slowing down to infuse those moments with love, gratitude, and purpose. These small, sweet acts create powerful shifts, bringing balance and peace to your space and, in turn, to your life. Remember, when you show up for your space, it shows up for you in return.

A Few of My Favorite Nestorations
1. Give your plants TLC
Plants bring fresh energy and life into your home. I love to water my plants and recite a mantra or phrase as I'm watering—maybe say "Love" or "Refresh." You can sing or talk to your plants. I also love to

name plants. Some are funny, some are serious, just like the energy of the plant. My money tree is "Theodore," and my Philodendron is of course "Phil." You might feel silly naming them, but try it!

2. Smooth Out Your Bed with Extra Care

If you already make your bed, you get a gold star. Making your bed each day sets the tone for your day. But slow it down, smoothing out the wrinkles on the duvet, fluff and adjust the trims on the pillows as you place them with care. Taking even two extra minutes when making your bed to really give it love will make a difference. Your whole day will feel grounded.

3. Sweep as an Energetic Reset

Sweeping your floors probably feels like it falls into the "chore" category, but when you approach this act as a Nestoration, it takes on a whole new energy. You're not just removing dirt but also stagnant energy. Once you sweep, you'll be able to connect with the earth and ground much easier. No one feels grounded with debris, food crumbs, and pet hair between their feet and the earth. And yes, I have a Roomba too. What a lifesaver some days! If this is you, I especially want you to squeeze in a few moments to sweep. With each stroke of my broom, I like to recite, "I invite in love, peace, joy, and harmony into my home." This might sound "woo," but give it a try. You might be surprised how uplifting it is.

4. Light a Candle with Intention

You might reach for the nearest candle and your quick flick-n-flame to get rid of last night's lingering dinner smells (and, of course, I always recommend choosing a healthier, non-toxic candle). But did you know that the moment you light a candle, the energy in your space shifts? That tiny spark is a powerful moment, one you can make the most of with just a little intention.

Instead of using the same lighter you'd grab for your grill or firepit, elevate the experience by choosing a beautiful box of matches. As you strike the match, hold a wish, dream, or intention in your mind. Feel that spark, both literally and energetically as you light your candle. This is a simple but powerful way to weave magic and intention into your morning—or anytime.

5. Let Fresh Air Flow

If you live in the northern part of the country like I do, you know that feeling when spring begins to tease us, hinting that she's on her way. Those unexpected, gorgeous days sneak in, and suddenly, we're itching to swap the treadmill for a refreshing walk outside, soaking up every bit of sunshine we can get. While you have the urge to get outside and experience the warm sun and fresh air, so does your home.

Open the windows and allow fresh air to flow in and stagnant air from the winter months to flow out. Additionally, opt for a once-a-week fresh air reset. No matter the time of year, hot or cold, I go through my home and crack the windows for a minute to encourage the fresh air to flow in and out. Don't overthink the electric bills; just a few moments won't make that much of a difference.

This practice will be helpful especially if you're in a newer home or have newer furniture. Everything from furniture framing to the cushions, mattresses, and even building materials and that new rug you just rolled out in your foyer is likely off-gassing, the release of chemicals after unboxing or installing items in your home. You'll notice you're being affected by them if you're feeling foggy, irritable or light-headed. Also, brand new homes are built incredibly tight. While that might sound initially better when we get our mid-summer electric bills, any off-gassing and stagnant air has nowhere to go. Each time you open your windows for some fresh air, visualize the old air flowing out and clean air flowing in.

Your home is a living, breathing extension of you. When you approach these daily tasks with presence and love, they stop feeling like obligations and start feeling like beautiful, sacred rituals. Each small Nestoration is a significant opportunity to elevate your home and lift your mood.

CHAPTER 25

The Home Within You

YOUR BODY REFLECTS
YOUR ENVIRONMENT

Most people don't realize how deeply their surroundings influence the body. Sure, you might realize you prefer one person's home over another or you gravitate toward one room in your space over another, but have you ever stopped to think how it's influencing your body?

The energy between your home and body is reciprocal. The energy of your body feeds off your home, and the energy of your home feeds off your body. When the two are in harmony, you'll feel it.

THE HOME—BODY DISCONNECT: TWO STORIES

Grace

My client Grace had been walking nearly 10,000 steps every day and began avoiding her Friday night fast-food dinners in pursuit of better health. When I arrived at her home, though, she was sitting on her sofa in tears. I saw she hadn't addressed the five cardboard boxes in her dining room that we'd discussed months before. "Why do I still feel so depressed every night? she asked me. "I'm making healthier choices!"

I could sense her frustration and gently reminded her of the boxes. I told her, "You can do all these great things for your body, but if you don't tend to your home, you'll still be out of sync." The boxes contained paperwork from her sister who had passed nearly ten years ago. Compassionately, I explained that holding onto these boxes was keeping her stuck. She could be making healthy choices for her body, but until she took on the task of caring for the boxes and their contents, she'd still feel stuck.

Gary

Gary, a previous client who had hired me to help stage his home for sale, invited me to his new condo in a trendy, up-and-coming neighborhood. He loved the energy of the area and, with his keen eye for style, had filled his home with mid-century modern touches. Despite putting so much thought into crafting a space he loved, Gary admitted he still felt constantly stressed and exhausted.

After a tour of his new condo, I saw the culprit: his kitchen. The kitchen was filled with all the wrong things: frozen pizzas, tons of processed food, and lots of alcohol. There wasn't a vegetable in sight.

I explained to Gary, just as I had to Grace, that the energy is all reciprocal. I encouraged Gary to stock up on healthy foods he enjoyed and keep them easily accessible. He also decided to try a healthy food delivery service. And I suggested he put the alcohol behind a cabinet door and replace the display with a coffee station or a simple, beautiful carafe of water and pretty glasses. With just a few tweaks, he started making better food choices, which made his body feel better and move into alignment with his home.

ENERGY HYGIENE: CLEANSING YOUR FIELD

Sometimes we need to intentionally cleanse the energy of our bodies for balance. You may have heard of this as "energy hygiene," tending to your energetic field, releasing what's not yours while restoring yourself back to a peaceful state.

A few easy options to practice:

- Take a weekly salt bath to draw out energetic residue.

- Mist a few sprays of a cleansing spritz around your body.

- Try a quick visualization where you imagine any stuck or heavy energy washing away.

These small, mindful practices not only protect your energy but help you move through your day feeling clearer, grounded, and supported.

MY FAVORITE ENERGY HYGIENE PRACTICES

1. Dry brushing

Dry brush before each shower to exfoliate and stimulate lymph flow.

2. Oil Massage

(Ayurvedic Abhyanga) is a practice that I learned from my Ayurvedic practitioner, Lauren. It's a lovely ritual that I take on one evening a week. It's not only a beautiful ceremony of self-care but is also incredibly relaxing and nourishing. Afterward, I sleep like a baby!

3. Intentional Hydration

I start every morning with drinking a full glass of room temperature water and end my day with another. Hydration to begin and end the day feels right to me. This is in addition to anything I may normally drink during the day. I sip this while looking out at the trees in the backyard and getting grounded.

4. Meditation

The best time for my meditation is around 9 AM. Some people say you must meditate first thing in the morning, but this fits my schedule and feels natural. Take on meditation when it feels most natural to you.

Your body is an extension of your home, and your home, an extension of your body. Nurturing one supports the other. The changes don't need to be dramatic. Just a few intentional steps—clearing out a space, stocking nourishing food, and tending to your body—can bring the balance you've been craving.

Coming Home

WHAT IF YOUR HOME COULD BE MORE than just a place to live? What if it could be a mirror, a sanctuary, a partner in your growth?

You've traveled through this book chapter by chapter, room by room, exploring holistic design, Feng Shui, and the deeper meaning behind your surroundings. My hope is that you now see your home—and yourself—through a more intuitive, compassionate lens.

COMING HOME IS NOT
ABOUT PERFECTION

Coming home is not about perfectly curated shelves or spotless counters. It's about true alignment, support, and that deep exhale at the end of the day. It's about surrounding yourself with reminders of your next steps and who you're becoming.

You've discovered how your environment reflects your internal world, how clutter holds emotions, how color stirs memory, how sound and scent influence your nervous system. You've also explored your space with your new lenses.

Now, as we close this journey together, I want to remind you ...

YOU ARE MAGIC

Crystals, mirrors, or perfectly styled pillows don't shift energy—your intention, attention, and willingness to experiment do. Remember, your decision to claim a bit of beauty, harmony, and peace within your four walls is an act of self-respect and self-love, a statement to the world that you *are* worthy of a life that feels good.

So, take on what resonated. Release what didn't. Try a little. Experiment. Reflect. Then try again. Be curious about what sticks.

Your home will keep whispering to you. You only need to listen with open ears and an open heart.

So, here's to fresh flowers on the table and to coming home not just to a space but to yourself.

I hope you leave these pages inspired, supported, and most of all ... at home.

XOXO,

Lisa

KEEP THE ENERGY FLOWING

Your journey with Feng Shui and holistic design doesn't end here. Let's keep the good chi flowing!

Work with me: purelivingwithlisamorton.com
Learn from me: elevatedlivingschool.com

Our holistic design courses and Feng Shui certifications give you the skills and insights to create spaces that inspire harmony and wellness. Join us for a class.

Listen: *Feng Shui Living: Tips for Busy Women* (Podcast)
Watch: *Feng Shui Living: Tips for Busy Women* (YouTube)

Find me on Instagram, Facebook & Pinterest:
@Purelivingwithlisamorton @Fengshuilivingpodcast
@Elevatedlivingschool

And if you love a supportive community, join my private Facebook group: **The Good Chi Club.**

Let's continue this journey together—creating spaces that feel beautiful, balanced, and full of love.

ACKNOWLEDGMENTS

THIS BOOK IS THE RESULT OF YEARS of listening—to homes, to energy, and to people's stories—and I could not have written it without the guidance, love, and support I've received along the way.

To my husband, who has supported me through every chapter (in life and in this book).

Thank you for your patience and belief in my work—even when it meant moving furniture again. I promise I won't make you move too much more!

To my clients, my students, and community.

Thank you for trusting me with your homes and your life stories. You've inspired so much of what is on these pages. It's been an honor.

To my mentors and teachers in Feng Shui, holistic design, and energy work.

I am forever grateful for your wisdom. Specifically, LuAnn Cibik, you've given me a magnificent lens through which to see the world and a beautiful language to share it. I can't thank you enough.

To my amazing assistant and dear friend, Maggie Kitch. You are my bright full moon. Your presence, intuition, and unwavering support have carried me through more phases than you know. I'm so grateful for you.

To my writing coach and editor, Gail Kerzner, The Savvy Red Pen, who cheered me on and reminded me to keep going when I got frustrated or frozen.

Thank you for holding space for me creatively and personally. You not only helped me write a book I love but also helped me grow as an individual through my writing.

And finally, to the homes themselves. Thank you for speaking. I hope this book helps more people learn to listen to what you have to say.

ABOUT THE AUTHOR

LISA MORTON is the founder of *Pure Living with Lisa Morton*, a thriving holistic design and Feng Shui consultancy devoted to helping people create homes that feel good, flow beautifully, and support their deepest intentions. With over 20 years of experience in the interior  design industry, Lisa has guided countless individuals in transforming their spaces into sanctuaries of well-being, clarity, and joy.

A Midwest farm girl at heart, Lisa's early connection to nature planted the seeds for her signature approach—blending natural elements, soulful intention, and energetic alignment. Today, she channels that lifelong love of the land into creating interiors that not only look beautiful but also promote harmony, and a deep sense of home.

She is the host of the *Feng Shui Living Podcast* and a passionate speaker, teacher, and intuitive guide. Whether through her consultations, courses, or community offerings, Lisa's work invites others to come home to themselves, through the spaces they live in.

To cultivate balance in her own life, she enjoys exercise, reading books on health and wellness, and walks in the woods with her husband, Don, and their two English Mastiffs, Cub and Violet.

www.ingramcontent.com/pod-product-compliance
Lightning Source LLC
Chambersburg PA
CBHW021102130626
46554CB00002B/491